# HARD TO
# BELIEVE

OTHER BOOKS BY JOHN MACARTHUR

*Twelve Extraordinary Women*

*The Book on Leadership*

*Twelve Ordinary Men*

*Safe in the Arms of God*

*The MacArthur New Testament Commentary Series*

*Successful Christian Parenting*

*The Freedom and Power of Forgiveness*

*The MacArthur Study Bible*

*Strength for Today*

*The Glory of Heaven*

*The Vanishing Conscience*

*Reckless Faith*

*The Miracle of Christmas*

*Anxiety Attacked*

*The Gospel According to the Apostles*

*Drawing Near*

*Ashamed of the Gospel*

*Rediscovering Expository Preaching*

*Charismatic Chaos*

*Our Sufficiency in Christ*

*The Gospel According to Jesus*

# HARD TO BELIEVE

### THE HIGH COST AND INFINITE VALUE
### OF FOLLOWING JESUS

# JOHN MACARTHUR

**NELSON BOOKS**
A Division of Thomas Nelson Publishers
*Since 1798*

www.thomasnelson.com

Published in Nashville, Tennessee, by Thomas Nelson, Inc.

Nelson Books may be purchased in bulk for educational, business,
fundraising, or sales promotional use. For information, please email
SpecialMarkets@ThomasNelson.com.

Published in association with the literary agency of Wolgemuth & Associates, Inc.
Unless otherwise noted, Scripture quotations are from THE NEW KING JAMES
VERSION. Copyright © 1979, 1980, 1982, Thomas Nelson, Inc., Publishers.

Scriptures noted KJV are from THE KING JAMES VERSION.

**Library of Congress Cataloging-in-Publication Data**

MacArthur, John, 1939–
    Hard to believe : the high cost and infinite value of following Jesus / John
MacArthur.
        p. cm.
    Includes bibliographical references.
    ISBN 0-7852-8798-1 (trape paper)
    ISBN 0-7852-6345-4 (hardcover)
    1. Christian life. I. Title.
    BV4501.3.M2 2003
    248.4—dc22

                                                        2003019724

*Printed in the United States of America*
06 07 08 09 RRD 5 4 3

band," and that those who come will, "believe it or not, even have fun." That's all great if you're a coffeehouse. But anyone who claims to be calling people to the gospel of Jesus with those as his priorities is calling them to a lie.

It's Christianity for consumers: Christianity Lite, the redirection, watering down, and misinterpretation of the biblical gospel in an attempt to make it more palatable and popular. It tastes great going down and settles light. It seems to salve your feelings and scratch your itch; it's custom-tailored to your preferences. But that lightness will never fill you up with the true, saving gospel of Jesus Christ, because it is designed by man and not God, and it is hollow and worthless. In fact, it's worse than worthless, because people who hear the message of Christianity Lite think they're hearing the gospel— think they're being rescued from eternal judgment—when, in fact, they're being tragically misled.

## THE FALSE GOSPEL OF SELF-ESTEEM

The true gospel is a call to self-denial. It is not a call to self-fulfillment. And that puts it in opposition to the contemporary evangelical gospel, where ministers view Jesus as a utilitarian genie. You rub the lamp, and He jumps out and says you have whatever you want; you give Him your list and He delivers.

Defending the true gospel has put me in pretty serious opposition to folks who don't want to take the Bible seriously. I always say that the people I pastor at Grace Church must have a heart to submit to the Word of God, because that's the message they're going to get, unadorned and unadulterated, every time they walk through the door. If they're not willing to face the hard truth of conviction over their sins, the hard disturbing reality of self-denial, and the hard demands of following Christ, they're not going to hang around very long.

# 1

## TASTES GREAT, LESS FILLING

The first role of successful merchandising is to give consumers what they want. If they want bigger burgers, make their burgers bigger. Designer bottled water in six fruit flavors? Done. Minivans with ten cup holders? Give them twenty. You've got to keep the customer satisfied. You've got to modify your product and your message to meet their needs if you want to build a market and get ahead of the competition.

Today this same consumer mind-set has invaded Christianity. The church service is too long, you say? We'll shorten it (one pastor guarantees his sermons will never last more than seven minutes!). Too formal? Wear your sweatsuit. Too boring? Wait'll you hear our band!

And if the message is too confrontational, or too judgmental, or too exclusive, scary, unbelievable, hard to understand, or too much anything else for your taste, churches everywhere are eager to adjust that message to make you more comfortable. This new version of Christianity makes you a partner on the team, a design consultant on church life, and does away with old-fashioned authority, guilt trips, accountability, and moral absolutes.

One suburban church sent out a mailer recently, promising an "informal, relaxed, casual atmosphere," "great music from our

# HARD TO BELIEVE

It's not my truth. I don't have any saving truth, neither does anyone else but God. Here's your most critical opportunity in all eternity—to hear what He has written about the way to heaven.

That's enough introduction. If you are still interested, get ready to be set free from the search for truth—here it comes from God's Word.

—JOHN MACARTHUR

# INTRODUCTION

In this space, it is the ordinary duty of the author to introduce what's coming in the book. Fair enough.

Do you want to be forgiven of all your sins, freed from judgment and eternal punishment, to be rescued from Satan's power to become a beloved child of God, and to be lavishly enriched forever with wonders and astonishing experiences in the limitless joys of eternal heaven? That's the question. If your answer is no, give this book to someone else. If your answer is yes, know this: Many people—many, many, Jesus said, who answer a quick yes won't ever receive what their yes wants.

You can want God's love, grace, forgiveness, blessing, and the inconceivable bliss of heaven—you can want it badly—and never get it.

Why so? Because you are misinformed about how. Does that make sense? The world is filled with millions of people who think they are headed for heaven—but they are deadly wrong. Probably most people think heaven awaits them, but it doesn't. But what is especially sad, is that many of those people sit in evangelical churches misinformed!

If you are still with me—and you want the truth for yourself and others—keep reading.

# CONTENTS

Introduction                                    ix

1. Tastes Great, Less Filling                    1

2. The Hard Truth                               19

3. Truth in a Privy Pot                         37

4. The Best Example                             53

5. Highway to Heaven                            73

6. Empty Words                                  93

7. The Rock of True Faith                      107

8. Hallmarks of Discipleship                   121

9. Can't Get No Satisfaction                   141

10. Traitors to the Faith                       159

11. Why We're Still Here                        183

12. But Some Will Believe                       201

Notes                                          217
Acknowledgments                                219
About the Author                               221

To Spencer Nilson,
my friend and fellow believer,
with enduring gratitude for your personal friendship
and encouragement, and your relentless passion
for the truth.

Some within the framework of evangelicalism will tell you Jesus just wants you well, and if you're not well, it's because you haven't turned in your spiritual lottery ticket. If you're not rich, it's because you haven't claimed it. Jesus wants you free from debt, and if you send the televangelists enough money, that act of faith will free you from the demon of debt. Your salvation through Christ is a guarantee of health, wealth, prosperity, and happiness.

The psychologically man-centered evangelicals tell you that Jesus gives you peace, Jesus gives you joy, Jesus makes you a better salesman, and Jesus helps you hit more home runs. Jesus really wants to make you feel better about yourself. He wants to elevate your self-image. He wants to put an end to your negative thinking.

It's interesting how this trend has come into the church. I've been around long enough to have seen it arrive. It blossomed, I think, most pointedly through the effort of the ever present small screen religious personality Robert Schuller and a book he wrote a number of years ago called *Self-Esteem: The New Reformation*. I reviewed that book for a national magazine. I thought Schuller's view was a turning point, literally, as the title says, an attempt to promote a new reformation. It was an effort to replace the biblical gospel with a new gospel. And it worked.

In that book, Robert Schuller attacked the Protestant Reformation. Calling for a new reformation he wrote: "It is precisely at this point that classical theology has erred in its insistence that theology be 'God-centered' and not 'man-centered.'"[1] So, according to Schuller, the first thing we have to do is put an end to classical, God-centered theology and replace it with man-centered theology.

To define man-centered theology (an oxymoron), he wrote further, "This master plan of God is designed around the deepest needs of human beings—self-dignity, self-respect, self-worth, self-esteem."[2] For Schuller, the pearl of great price is self-respect and self-esteem.

He went on to say, "Success is to be defined as the gift of self-esteem that God gives us as a reward for our sacrificial service in building self-esteem in others. Win or lose: If we follow God's plan as faithfully as we can, we will feel good about ourselves. That is success!"[3]

Pardon me if I don't join. I can't think of a plan with which I'd less like to associate.

In this new reformation of self-esteem, the first thing required is to pull God down from His supremely elevated place so you can then lift yourself up, replacing God-exalting theology with man-exalting self-esteem psychology. To pull this off requires altering and misinterpreting the Bible and the gospel for the grand purpose of making people feel better about themselves, so they can fulfill their dreams and realize their visions.

Maybe the most amazing statement in *Self-Esteem: The New Reformation* is the following: "Once a person believes he is an 'unworthy sinner,' it is doubtful if he can really honestly accept the saving grace God offers in Jesus Christ."[4] So, if you want to be saved, according to this new gospel you cannot believe yourself to be an unworthy sinner. How twisted is that? How contrary to the truth is that? But it is just the sort of man-centered, self-esteem gospel that eventually became the seeker-friendly movement, which has hijacked so many churches. It's a kind of quasi-Christian narcissism, or self-love, that is characteristic of false teachers: according to 2 Timothy 3, which reminds us, "Dangerous times will come, for men will be lovers of themselves" (see 2 Tim. 3:1–2).

Christianity, in the hands of some seeker-sensitive church leaders, has become a "get what you want" rather than a "give up everything" movement. These leaders have prostituted the divine intention of the gospel. They have replaced the glory of God with the satisfaction of man. They have traded the concept of abandoning our lives to the honor of Christ for Christ honoring us. As such, our submission to His will is replaced by His submission to our will.

Since people usually reject the real gospel, modern evangelicals have simply changed the message.

A saint of many centuries ago got it right with this prayer:

> Lord, high and holy, meek and lowly, let me learn by paradox that the way down is the way up, that to be low is to be high, that the broken heart is the healed heart, that the contrite spirit is the rejoicing spirit, that the repenting soul is the victorious soul, that to have nothing is to possess everything, that to bear the cross is to wear the crown, that to give is to receive. Let me find thy light in my darkness, thy joy in my sorrow, thy grace in my sin, thy riches in my poverty, thy glory in my valley, thy life in my death.[5]

"Thy life in my death"? That's the true gospel. Jesus said it unmistakably and inescapably, "If anyone desires to come after Me, let him deny himself, and take up his cross, and follow Me. For whoever desires to save his life will lose it, but whoever loses his life for My sake will find it" (Matt. 16:24–25). It's not about exalting me, it's about *slaying* me. It's the death of self. You win by losing; you live by dying. And that is the heart message of the gospel. That is the essence of discipleship.

The passage mentions nothing about improving your self-esteem, being rich and successful, feeling good about yourself, or having your felt needs met, which is what so many churches are preaching these days in order to sugarcoat the truth.

So who's right? Is the message of Christianity self-fulfillment, or is it self-denial? It can't be both. If it's just a matter of opinion, I'll do my thing and you do yours, and we'll both cruise contentedly along in separate directions. But Christianity, the genuine gospel of Jesus Christ, is not a matter of opinion. It is a matter of truth. What you want, or I want, or anybody else wants, makes no difference whatsoever. It is what it is—by God's sovereign will.

## THE HARD WORDS OF JESUS

I have no idea how the fans of Christianity Lite reconcile their approach to religion with the teachings of Jesus, or how they become comfortable ignoring what He said. But the only acceptable approach—for me and you—is to take our Lord at His word in the single source of truth for every authentic Christian: the word of God revealed in the Bible. So let's go there.

Luke 9 cuts to the core of the question of what Christianity is all about. Here, Jesus was with his disciples shortly after miraculously feeding a crowd of five thousand, who had come to hear him speak, with one modest basket of loaves and fishes. In Luke 9:23–26 we read:

> Then He said to them all, "If anyone desires to come after Me, let him deny himself, and take up his cross daily, and follow Me. For whoever desires to save his life will lose it, but whoever loses his life for My sake will save it. For what profit is it to a man if he gains the whole world, and is himself destroyed or lost? For whoever is ashamed of Me and My words, of him the Son of Man will be ashamed when He comes in His own glory, and in His Father's, and of the holy angels."

It's pretty simple. Anyone who wants to come after Jesus into the kingdom of God—anyone who wants to be a Christian—has to face three commands: 1) deny himself, 2) take up his cross daily, and 3) follow Him. These words are hard to believe. They're not consumer-friendly or seeker-sensitive. Christianity Lite is nowhere to be found. But this is not an obscure passage, or something different from other teachings of Jesus. These are principles that He taught consistently and repeatedly throughout His ministry, over and over again in all different settings.

This is not news. When Martin Luther launched the Protestant Reformation in 1517 by posting his Ninety-five Theses on the door at Wittenberg, he affirmed in the fourth thesis that salvation required self-hate. He wrote that "self-hate remains right up to entrance into the kingdom of heaven." The original Greek word for "deny" means "to refuse to associate with." The thought is that if you want to be Christ's disciple, and receive forgiveness and eternal life, you must refuse to associate any longer with the person you are! You are sick of your sinful self and want nothing to do with you anymore. And it may mean not just you, but your family.

In Matthew 10:32, Jesus talked about confessing Him as Lord and Savior: "Therefore whoever confesses Me before men, him I will also confess before My Father who is in heaven." And then in verses 34–36: "Do not think that I came to bring peace on the earth. I did not come to bring peace but a sword. For I have come to set a man against his father, a daughter against her mother, and a daughter-in-law against her mother-in-law; and 'a man's enemies will be those of his own household.'"

It's not a friendly invitation; it's a warning: If you come to Christ, it may make your family worse, not better. It may send a rift into your family, the likes of which you have never experienced before. If you give your life to Jesus Christ, there will be an impassable gulf between you and people who don't give their lives to Him. In fact, as the New Age Hindu mystic Deepak Chopra said to me on CNN Television: "You and I are in two different universes." I replied that he was exactly right. And that is not just true for strangers but also for family members, creating a severe breach in those most intimate of all relationships.

Verse 37 adds, "He who loves father or mother more than Me is not worthy of Me. And he who loves son or daughter more than Me is not worthy of Me." If you're not willing to pay the price of a permanent split in your family unless your loved ones come to Christ—

if you're not willing to pay the price of greater trauma, greater conflict, greater suffering in your family—then you're not worthy to be Jesus' disciple.

Verse 38: "And he who does not take his cross and follow after Me is not worthy of Me." Wait a minute. In Jesus' time, people associated a cross with one thing and one thing alone: a cross was an instrument of death. He was saying that if you're not willing to have conflict with the world to the degree that it could cost you your life, then you're not worthy of Him.

Verse 39: "He who finds his life will lose it, and he who loses his life for My sake will find it." This is an echo of Luke 9. It's about losing your life. It's not a man-centered theology, it's a Christ-centered theology that says, "I give everything to Christ, no matter what it costs me, even if it costs me my life."

## THE TRUE GOSPEL OF SCRIPTURE

This is a bedrock truth of Christianity that the Bible confirms repeatedly. Jesus said the same thing in many different ways. He said it in the familiar story of the rich young ruler. In Mark 10:17 the young synagogue leader ran up to Jesus, knelt before Him, and asked, "Good Teacher, what shall I do that I may inherit eternal life?"

What a setup for personal evangelism! Jesus could have said, "Pray this prayer" or "Make a decision to accept Me!" He didn't. Instead He confronted the young man with the reality of sin to reveal whether or not he was convicted of his wickedness and penitent over his iniquities. Jesus offered several of the Ten Commandments as examples of the law of God the young man had broken.

Rejecting any thought of sinfulness and repentance, the young man bragged about having obeyed the Ten Commandments all his life. He thought he was a perfect candidate for eternal life. But he got a response he didn't expect. In verse 21, Jesus said, "Go your way, sell whatever you have and give to the poor, and you will have treasure in heaven; and come, take up the cross, and follow Me." Jesus exposed his self-righteousness and then uncovered his love for money. The young ruler wanted Jesus to show him how to have eternal life. But Jesus told him that the price was giving up his illusion of self-righteousness, recognizing himself rather as an unworthy, wretched sinner. And he needed to be willing to submit to the Lord Jesus, even if it meant he had to give up all his earthly possessions. He might not ask, but the requirement for eternal life is the willingness to give it all up if He does.

The young man wouldn't do either—admit his sin or deny himself. As verse 22 tells us, "But he was sad at this word, and went away sorrowful, for he had great possessions." He decided he'd rather hold onto the deception of self-righteousness, and have his money and possessions, than have Jesus. He had no interest in self-denial, self-sacrifice, or submission. Therefore he was unworthy to be Jesus' disciple, and he himself shut the door to the kingdom of salvation.

We all know someone like the rich young ruler—cocky, self-assured, impressed with his own goodness—who sees Christian salvation as one more goal he can achieve through performance, skill, money, and influence. The Bible tells us that's not how it works. The goal is the unfamiliar one of sorrowfully acknowledging sin, of submission and sacrifice. If we're not willing to separate from our families, separate from the world, separate from the material things that we possess, then Jesus isn't that valuable to us. It's an all-or-nothing proposition.

There's yet another example in Luke 9:57, where Jesus was walking down the road with some of his followers, and one of them promised, "I will follow You wherever You go." Jesus didn't say, "Hey, that's great. We're all going to the Ritz-Carlton for caviar." What He said in verse 58 was, "Foxes have holes and the birds of the air have nests, but the Son of Man has nowhere to lay His head." Jesus didn't say, "Follow Me, and you will be happy, you will be healthy, wealthy, prosperous, and successful." He said, "Just know this: I don't have any place to lay My head. Discipleship is going to cost you whatever you have. Don't expect comfort and ease."

The story continues in verse 59: "Then He said to another, 'Follow Me.' But he said, 'Lord, let me go first and bury my father.'" The implication here was that his father wasn't even dead. What did he mean, "go first and bury" his father? Did he mean go to the funeral? No, he meant hang around until he got the inheritance! He wasn't going to have anything if he followed Jesus. Jesus had nothing to give him, so he wanted to stick around the house until he could pack a fortune in his bag and then come after Jesus. He disappeared too.

A third would-be follower of Jesus wanted to return home and organize a big farewell party with friends and family—to secure support for his venture. Jesus told him that those who entered His kingdom didn't go back to bring along elements of the old life. Rather they were like a farmer, who, once he grabbed the plow, kept looking forward so the furrow was straight (Luke 9:61–62).

Jesus set the standard as total self-denial. In Luke 14:26, a great multitude was following Him and He turned and spoke to them: "If anyone comes to Me"—meaning those who wanted to be His true followers—"and does not hate his father and mother, wife and children, brothers and sisters, yes, and his own life also, he cannot be My disciple." Self-hate? What a powerful truth! This is not salvation by good works but the very opposite: salvation by rejecting all hope of pleasing God on our own.

Following Jesus is not about you and me. Being a Christian is not about us; it's not about our self-esteem. It's about our being sick of our sin and our desperation for forgiveness. It is about seeing Christ as the priceless Savior from sin and death and hell, so that we willingly give up as much as it takes, even if it costs us our families, our marriages, and whatever else we cherish and possess.

It might even cost us our lives, as Jesus said in Luke 9:24 and reaffirmed in 14:27: "And whoever does not bear his cross"—that is, be willing to die and give his life—"and come after Me cannot be My disciple."

It can't be any clearer than that. If you try to hold onto you, your plan, your agenda, your success, your self-esteem, you lose forgiveness and heaven.

In John 12:24, Jesus said, "Most assuredly, I say to you, unless a grain of wheat falls into the ground and dies, it remains alone; but if it dies, it produces much grain." In other words, "If you're going to be fruitful in following Me," Jesus says, "it's going to cost you your life. You're going to have to die." Verse 25: "He who loves his life will lose it, and he who hates his life in this world will keep it for eternal life." The path that Jesus was going down was the path to persecution and death.

So you want to follow Jesus, do you? It'll cost you absolutely everything.

The Lord might not take your life. He might not take all your money. He might not take your family or your spouse. He might not take your job. But you need to be willing to give it all up, if that's what He asks. You need to be desperate enough to embrace Christ no matter what the price.

If you want to follow Christ right into heaven, here's the message: Deny yourself, take up your cross, and follow Him. Do you hear that in the contemporary gospel? Do you ever hear that in a message a television preacher or an evangelist gives? Do you ever hear anybody stand up in a crowd and say, "If you want to become a Christian, slay yourself! Refuse to associate any longer with yourself, reject all the things your self longs and wants and hopes for! Be willing to die for the sake of Christ, if required, and while living slavishly, submit in obedience to Jesus Christ!" That doesn't sell! That's not smart marketing.

It's a message that's hard to believe, because self-denial is so hard to do. It just happens to be the truth.

## THE NARROW GATE

So, what do you want to do? According to lots of churches and preachers, the answer is to popularize the gospel: get rid of all this slaying-yourself and carrying-your-cross stuff, and get a decent band up there on the stage. Tell everybody God wants him to be happy and successful and full of self-esteem.

The only problem is that saying those things gives people who don't know any better the illusion they're saved, when they're not. And someday, when they face Christ, they're going to say, "Lord, Lord!" and He's going to say, "Depart from Me. I never knew you" (see Matt. 7:23). What's a good band worth then? About as much as healthy self-esteem.

Mankind wants glory. We want health. We want wealth. We want happiness. We want all our felt needs met, all our little human itches scratched. We want a painless life. We want the crown without the cross. We want the gain without the pain. We want the words of Christian salvation to be easy.

That's how people think. But that's not God's instruction to us. According to Hebrews 2:10, suffering made perfect the Captain of our salvation. And so we also will go through the crucible of suffering. What we suffer first of all is the death of all hopes, all ambitions, all desires, all longings, all needs that are human.

Listening to a seeker-sensitive evangelical preacher today, we're likely to think it's easy to be a Christian. Just say these little words, pray this little prayer, and poof! you're in the club. According to the

Bible, it doesn't work that way. In Matthew 7:13 during the Sermon on the Mount, Jesus admonished His followers, "Enter by the narrow gate." The connotation of "narrow" here is *constricted*. It's a very, very tight squeeze. We can't carry anything through it; we come through with nothing.

A wide religious gate also exists, and I am saddened to think so many preachers, and so many churches, are leading people through it. They're saying, "You don't have to do all that hard stuff to get into heaven. We're open-minded and inclusive, and we think everybody who wants to, should get saved."

We've actually come to the point where people who call themselves Christians have *apologized* on behalf of all us hopelessly inflexible nitpickers: those who hang onto old, outmoded ideas that Christianity should be biblical, exclusive, inflexible, and inconvenient. Recently, a group of more than fifty pastors and laymen, including a divinity school dean, representing half a dozen mainline Christian denominations, placed an ad in a major daily newspaper insisting it was "wrong—ethically, morally, and spiritually—for anyone, whether individual, group, church, or religion, to claim *exclusive* access to God or God's grace, blessing, or salvation . . . Claims of exclusivity by Christians and others have played a self-justifying role in causing untold human suffering . . ."

Excuse me, but if Christians don't acknowledge and preach the fact that salvation is through Christ alone, they are herding unwitting people through the wide gate that leads to destruction. That's not my opinion; that's the Word of God. People are breezing through those wide, comfortable, inviting gates with all their baggage, their self-needs, their self-esteem, and their desire for fulfillment and self-satisfaction. And the most horrible thing about it is they think they're going to heaven. And somebody thinks he's done them a big favor by coming up with a consumer-friendly gospel about which everybody feels good.

But that gospel is a false gospel, a treacherous lie. That easy-access gate doesn't go to heaven. It says "Heaven," but it ends up in hell.

"Because narrow is the gate," Jesus said in Matthew 7:14, "and difficult is the way which leads to life, and there are few who find it." I agree that we have a hard time finding it, especially today. You could go to church after church after church and never find it. It's a very narrow gate.

The same teaching appears in Luke 13:23–24: "Then one said to Him, 'Lord, are there few who are saved?' And He said to them, 'Strive to enter through the narrow gate, for many, I say to you, will seek to enter and will not be able.'" It's hard to find, and it's hard to get through.

Why is it so hard to find today, and why is it so hard to get through? It's hard to find because so many churches have strayed from teaching the truth of the gospel. And it's even harder, once we've heard the truth, to submit to it. Man worships himself. He's his own god. What we need to tell people is not "Come to Christ and you'll feel better about yourself," or "Jesus wants to meet whatever your needs are." Jesus doesn't want to meet our needs—our worldly, earthly, human needs. He wants us to be willing to say, "I will abandon all the things I think I need for the sake of Christ."

It's hard to get through the narrow gate because it's so hard for us to deny ourselves. Jesus' first requirement in Luke 9 was for Christians to deny themselves, but that's just about impossible to do. Self-importance is the reigning reality in human fallenness: man is the master of his own soul, the captain of his own fate, the monarch of his own world.

To say he has to deny and slay himself is simply too much to swallow. Preach a gospel that doesn't include that, and people will flock around to get out of hell and into heaven. But start preaching the *true* gospel, the hard words of Jesus that call for total and absolute self-denial—the recognition that we're worthy of nothing, commendable for nothing, and that nothing in us is worth salvaging—and that's a lot less popular. Take it from someone who has been targeted on national television for saying this.

## COUNTING THE COST

In Luke 14:28–30, Jesus asked, "For which of you, intending to build a tower, does not sit down first and count the cost, whether he has enough to finish it—lest, after he has laid the foundation, and is not able to finish, all who see it begin to mock him, saying, 'This man began to build and was not able to finish.'"

If you're going to come to Christ, you're going to have to count the cost. Have you counted the cost? Do you even understand there's a price to pay? We know what the price is because, as we've already seen, the Bible tells us clearly, unequivocally, and repeatedly. The price is a willingness to hate your father and mother, if necessary, hate your own life, carry your cross, and come after Jesus. Nothing in the world must we hold so dear that we will forfeit Christ for it.

Continuing in verses 31–32: "Or what king, going to make war against another king, does not sit down first and consider whether he is able with ten thousand to meet him who comes against him with twenty thousand? Or else, while the other is still a great way off, he sends a delegation and asks conditions of peace." You either make peace with the enemy if you can't conquer him, or you make sure you've got the troops that you need to win the battle. In other words, Jesus was saying, "Don't come to Me unless you've counted the cost. And the price is self-denial, self-crucifixion, and self-submission."

In Luke 14:33, He delivered the point: "So likewise, whoever of you does not forsake all that he has cannot be My disciple." We're not going to get saved by dumping all our earthly goods, but we have to be willing to do so. That's how devoted we have to be to the cause of Christ. We will deny ourselves all of our worldly longings. We will even deny our own right to live, and give our lives, if need be, for the cause of Jesus Christ. We will submit to His will, following Him whatever He asks, whether He says we must lose these things or we can keep them. That's up to Him.

Jesus told two parables in Matthew 13, beginning with verse 44. He said, "The kingdom of heaven is like treasure hidden in a field, which a man found and hid; and for joy over it he goes and sells all that he has and buys that field." In the next verse, He told the story of a man who found a pearl of great price and sold all he had to buy it. The complete surrender of all possessions is the essence of salvation. It is, "I give up everything. I deny myself. I offer my life, both in terms of death, if need be, and in terms of obedience in life."

Earlier we saw those who insist that the pearl of great price in the Christian faith is "genuine respect and self-esteem." It is nothing of the sort. The pearl of great price, the treasure worth everything you and I possess, is the saving grace of Jesus Christ that we are hopelessly undeserving of, but that we can claim as our own by denying ourselves, picking up our cross daily, and following Him.

This is the message of the gospel. When you call people to Jesus, that's what you have to say.

## KEEPING THE CUSTOMER SATISFIED

Now comes the issue that's behind all the pop music and self-congratulation and "fun" that the seeker-sensitive churches promise: people aren't going to buy Christianity if it's that hard. If it doesn't meet their needs, they won't be interested. If they want six fruit flavors and you've got only two, you've lost them. They need Christianity that tastes great, and if it's less filling in the short run, well, we'll explain all the hard stuff later.

There's a name for that in the marketing world, and it's called bait and switch. You advertise a TV for a rock-bottom price, but when the consumer gets to the store, that particular model is unavailable. There's a more expensive one here, however, that's a lot like it. It's not what we promised you. In fact, what we promised never existed. The offer was a sham.

What happens at a seeker-sensitive church when somebody takes the bait? He thinks, "Hey, this Christianity thing is not hard at all. Meet nice people, hear an inspiring message and some cool music, get to heaven." But at some point the truth comes out. The hard words of Jesus come out: "It's not about you, it's about Me and sacrificing yourself to follow Me."

It's absolutely true that nobody's going to want to be a Christian under those circumstances, *unless the Spirit of God is working in his heart.* Unless the Spirit of God is doing the work of conviction, is awakening the dead heart, and generating faith, nothing's going to happen, *no matter what you do.* And then *only the true message of Jesus, connected with the work of the Spirit, will produce true salvation.* The fountain of grace will open and flow to the self-denying sinner. This is the very essence of grace. It is when we offer nothing in ourselves as worthy of salvation, but affirm our hatred of worthless self, that God grants us grace to rescue us from sin and hell.

We can't reinvent the gospel to suit ourselves, our own comfort and convenience. But that's what people are doing today. That's why I've written this book. If you modify the message to make Christianity more attractive, then what you have is not Christianity. I'm not promoting legalism in any form, only fidelity to Scripture, though some people have decided I'm sort of harsh and hard-nosed. One well-known evangelical friend thought he was complimenting me when he introduced me by saying, "This is John MacArthur, who is much nicer in person than he is in his books."

I smiled and said, "In person it's much easier to demonstrate the love of Christ."

Well-meaning congregations and pastors go to great lengths to steer around the teachings of Jesus that are hard to believe. They don't do it because they're sinister, or malicious, or consciously out to deceive anybody. They do it because good news is fun to deliver, but hard words aren't. Hard words are sometimes confusing and embarrassing; it's hard to make eye contact when you repeat some of them.

Christians don't know how to interpret and share the hard words of Jesus, so they skip over them. But delivering half the message is almost worse than delivering no message at all. All of what Jesus has to say is important. It's not up to us to decide what we'll pass on and what we'll try to hide.

My prayer is that this book will help you understand that the right invitation to Christianity is the one that's complete and transparent; that hiding the truth doesn't help but, in fact, infinitely hurts people; and that there are ways you can use the full dimension of the gospel to proclaim a powerful, compelling evangelical message that the Lord will bless.

# 2

## THE HARD TRUTH

Perhaps the dominant myth in the evangelical church today is that the success of Christianity depends on how popular it is, and that the kingdom of God and the glory of Christ somehow advance on the back of public favor. This is an age-old fantasy. I remember reading a quote from the apologist Edward John Carnell in Ian Murray's biography of the Welsh preacher David Martyn Lloyd-Jones. During the formative years of Fuller Theological Seminary, Carnell said regarding evangelicalism, "We need prestige desperately."

Christians have worked hard to position themselves in places of power within the culture. They seek influence academically, politically, economically, athletically, socially, theatrically, religiously, and every other way, in hopes of gaining mass media exposure. But then when they get that exposure—sometimes through mass media, sometimes in a very broad-minded church environment—they present a reinvented designer pop gospel that subtly removes all of the offense of the gospel and beckons people into the kingdom along an easy path. They do away with all that hard-to-believe stuff about self-sacrifice, hating your family, and so forth.

The illusion is that we can preach our message more effectively from lofty perches of cultural power and influence, and once we've got everybody's attention, we can lead more people to Christ by taking out the sting of the gospel and nurturing a user-friendly message. But to get to these lofty perches, "Christian" public figures water down and compromise the truth; then, to stay up there, they cave in to pressure to perpetuate false teaching so their audience will stay loyal. Telling the truth becomes an unwise career move.

Local church pastors are among the first to be seduced into using this designer gospel, crafted to fit the sinner's desire and carefully tweaked to overcome consumer resistance. They stylize church meetings to look, sound, feel, and smell like the world, in order to remove the sinner's resistance and lure him into the kingdom down an easy and familiar path.

The idea is to make Christianity easy to believe. But the unvarnished, untweaked, unmodified, unavoidable truth is that the gospel is actually hard to believe. In fact, if the sinner is left to himself, it is absolutely impossible.

This is the pop philosophy: "If they like us, they'll like Jesus." The whole scheme works superficially, but only if we compromise the truth. And we can't just pick on the local preachers for reinventing the gospel, because they're acting no differently than the big-name televangelists and other more widely known evangelicals. To maintain their positions of power and influence, once they've achieved them, to maintain this tenuous alliance with the world in the name of love, attractiveness, and tolerance, and to keep the unconverted happy in church, they must replace the truth with something soothing and inoffensive. In fact, as a Calvinist once said, "Sometimes we don't present the gospel well enough for the non-elect to reject it."

Now, I don't want you to misunderstand me. I am committed to reaching as far as possible here and around the world to spread the gospel. I prefer righteousness to prevail over sin. I prefer to elevate righteous people and expose sin for what it really is, in all of its destructiveness. I long to see the glory of God extend to the ends of the earth. I long to see divine light flood the kingdom of darkness. No loyal child of God is ever content with sin, immorality, unrighteousness, error, or unbelief. The reproach that falls on the Lord falls on me, and zeal for His house eats me up, as it did David and as it did Jesus.

I hate the churches of the world, however, that have become havens for heretics. I resent a TV church that, in many cases, has become a den of thieves. I would love to see the divine Lord take a whip and have at it in the religion of our time. I sometimes pray imprecatory psalms directly on the heads of certain people. But mostly, I pray for the kingdom to come. Mostly I pray for the gospel to penetrate the hearts of the lost. I understand why John Knox said, "Give me Scotland or I die. What else do I live for?" I understand why pioneer missionary Henry Martyn ran out of a Hindu temple exclaiming, "I cannot endure existence if Jesus is to be so dishonored!"

I was on a radio talk show at a big station in a big city, where the host was a popular "Christian counselor." She had a three-hour show every weekday, advising listeners who called in about all sorts of problems, some of them very serious. By the kind of questions she asked me on the show, I figured she hadn't done a lot of reading about Christian doctrine. Off the air, during a commercial break, she said to me, "You use the word 'sanctification.' What exactly does that mean?"

That was a hint. If she didn't know what sanctification meant, she had some homework to do. We were still off the air, so I asked her, "How did you become a Christian?" I will never forget her answer. She said, "It was cool. One day I got Jesus' phone number and we've been connected ever since."

"What?" I asked, trying not to appear too incredulous. "What do you mean by that?"

"What do you mean, 'What do I mean by that?'" she shot back brusquely.

She didn't understand that her "testimony" even needed an explanation. Then she asked, "How did you become a Christian?" I started going briefly through the gospel. She stopped me and said, "Oh, come on! You don't have to go through all that, do you?"

Yes, you do.

I've made no truce with the way the world is. I resent everything that dishonors the Lord. I'm against everything He's against and for everything He supports. I long to see people brought to saving faith in Jesus Christ. I hate the fact that sinners die without any hope. I'm committed to the proclamation of the gospel. I'm not narrow in that sense. I want to be a little part of fulfilling the Great Commission. I want to preach the gospel to every creature.

It's not that I'm not interested in the lost of the world, or that I have made an easy truce with a wretched, sinful world that dishonors my God and Christ. The only question for me is, How do I do my part? What is my responsibility? It certainly can't be to compromise the message. The message is not mine, it's from God, and it is by that message that He saves.

Not only can I not compromise the message, I can't compromise the cost. I can't change the terms. We know Jesus said, "If you want to come after Me, deny yourself" (see Luke 9:23). Jesus said we have to take up our crosses all the way to death, if that's what He asks. I can't help it if that gospel offends a society awash in self-love. And I know this: the preaching of the truth truly influences the world and genuinely changes one soul at a time. And that happens only by the life-giving, light-sending, soul-transforming power of the Holy Spirit, in perfect fulfillment of the eternal plan of God. Your opinion or my opinion is not part of the equation.

The kingdom does not advance by human cleverness. It does not advance because we have gained positions of power and influence in the culture. It doesn't advance thanks to media popularity or opinion polls. It doesn't advance on the back of public favor. The kingdom of

God advances by the power of God alone, in spite of public hostility. When we truly proclaim it in its fullness, the saving message of Jesus Christ is, frankly, outrageously offensive. We proclaim a scandalous message. From the world's perspective, the message of the cross is shameful. In fact, it is so shameful, so antagonizing, and so offensive that even faithful Christians struggle to proclaim it, because they know it will bring resentment and ridicule.

## EMBARRASSED BY JESUS

I'm sure you've noticed, as I have, how hard it is for Christians on television or in the public eye to say the name "Jesus." Even well-known evangelical leaders avoid the word when speaking to a wide audience, not to mention "cross," "sin," "hell," and other foundational terms of the faith. They talk a lot about faith in a general, unattached sort of way, yet they shy away from any statement that requires them to take a stand.

In the wake of the terrorist attacks on September 11, 2001, many Americans instinctively sought courage and solace in Christ. But even then, in a service at the National Cathedral in Washington, D.C., broadcast live around the world, a Christian clergyman offered a prayer in the name of Jesus Christ but "respecting all religions." All religions? Druids? Cat worshippers? Witches? A Christian minister in a Christian church shouldn't feel compelled to qualify or apologize for praying to the one true Savior.

Paul made a remarkable statement in Romans 1:16–17: "For I am not ashamed of the gospel of Christ, for it is the power of God to salvation for everyone who believes, for the Jew first and also for the Greek. For in it the righteousness of God is revealed from faith to faith; as it is written, 'The just shall live by faith.'"

Now why would Paul say, "I'm not ashamed of the gospel"? Who would ever be ashamed of such good news? Would someone who had found the cure for AIDS have to overcome immense shame to proclaim it? Would a person who had discovered a cure for cancer have to get over terrible shame to be able to open his mouth? Why is the cross so hard to mention?

Even though Paul's message of salvation was the greatest and most important message in history, audiences and authorities had treated him shamefully for preaching it, time and again. By this point in his ministry they had imprisoned him in Philippi (Acts 16:23–24), chased him out of Thessalonica (Acts 17:10), smuggled him out of Berea (Acts 17:14), laughed at him in Athens (Acts 17:32), branded him a fool in Corinth (1 Cor. 1:18, 23), and stoned him in Galatia (Acts 14:19). He had every reason to feel ashamed, yet his enthusiasm for the gospel was undiminished. And he never, for a moment, considered watering it down to make it more appealing to his audiences.

At some point or other in our Christian lives, we have all been ashamed and kept our mouths closed when we should have opened them. Or, given the chance, we've hidden behind some sort of innocuous "Jesus loves you and wants to make you happy" message. If you have never felt shame in proclaiming the gospel, it's probably because you haven't proclaimed the gospel clearly, in its entirety, the way Jesus proclaimed it.

Why can't the Christian business executive witness to his board of directors? Why can't the Christian university professor stand up before the whole faculty and proclaim the gospel? We all want to be accepted—yet we know, as Paul discovered so many times, that we have a message the world will reject, and the stronger we hold to that message, the more hostile the world becomes. So we begin to feel the shame. Paul rose above that by the grace of God and the power of the Spirit, and he said, "I'm not ashamed." It's a striking example for us, because he knew the price of fidelity to the truth: public rejection, imprisonment, and ultimately, execution.

Human nature really hasn't changed much throughout history;

shame and honor were as big a deal in the ancient world as they are today. Back in the ninth century B.C., the epic poet Homer wrote, "The chief good was to be well spoken of, the chief evil, to be badly spoken of by one's society." In the first century A.D., the apostle Paul "ministered in a shame-sensitive, honor-seeking culture," shamelessly preaching a shameful message about a publicly shamed person.[1] And so the message was offensive. It was scandalous. It was stupid. It was foolish. It was moronic.

Yet, as 1 Corinthians 1:21 says, "it pleased God through the foolishness of the message preached to save those who believe." It was this scandalous, offensive, foolish, ridiculous, bizarre, absurd message of the cross that God used to save those who believe. Roman authorities executed His Son, the Lord of the world, by a method they reserved only for the dregs of society; His followers had to be faithful enough to risk meeting the same shameful end.

## THE SHAME OF THE CROSS[2]

We preach a shameful message when we preach of Jesus on the cross. Being crucified was a degrading insult, and the idea of worshipping someone who had been crucified was absolutely unimaginable. Of course, we don't see people being crucified now as Paul's listeners did in the first century, so the impact is somewhat lost on us. But Paul knew what he was up against: "For the message of the cross is foolishness to those who are perishing" (1 Cor. 1:18); "For Jews request a sign, and Greeks seek after wisdom; but we preach Christ crucified, to the Jews a stumbling block and to the Greeks foolishness" (vv. 22–23). The message of the cross is foolishness, *moria* in Greek, from which we get the word "moron."

Verses 22 and 23 tell us the Jews were looking for a sign. "You're the Messiah," they said to Jesus, "so give us a sign." They were expecting some great supernatural wonder that would identify and attract them to the promised Messiah. They wanted something flashy. Even though Jesus had given them miracle after miracle during His ministry, they wanted some sort of supermiracle they could all look at and say, "That's the sign! That's the proof that this is the Messiah at last!"

The Greeks, on the other hand, weren't so much interested in the miraculous. They weren't looking for a supernatural sign; they were looking for wisdom. They wanted to validate a true religion through some transcendental insight, some elevated idea, some esoteric knowledge, some sort of spiritual experience, maybe even an out-of-body experience or another imaginary emotional event.

The Greeks wanted wisdom, and the Jews wanted a sign. God gave them exactly the opposite. The Jews received a *skandalon*, a crucified Messiah—scandalous, blasphemous, bizarre, offensive, unbelievable. And for the Greeks who were looking for esoteric knowledge, something high and noble and lofty, all this nonsense about the eternal Creator God of the universe being crucified was idiotic.

From both the Greek and Roman points of view, the stigma of crucifixion made the whole notion of the gospel claiming Jesus as the Messiah an absolute absurdity. A glance at the history of crucifixion in first-century Rome reveals what Paul's contemporaries thought about it. It was a horrific form of capital punishment, originating, most likely, in the Persian Empire, but other barbarians used it as well. The condemned died an agonizingly slow death by suffocation, gradually becoming too exhausted and traumatized to pull himself up on the nails in his hands, or push himself up on the nail through his feet, enough to take a deep breath of air. King Darius crucified three thousand Babylonians. Alexander the Great crucified two thousand from the city of Tyre. Alexander Janius crucified eight hundred Pharisees, while they watched soldiers slaughter their wives and children at their feet.

This sealed the horror of the crucifixion in the Jewish mind. Romans came to power in Israel in 63 B.C. and used crucifixion extensively. Some writers say authorities crucified as many as thirty thousand people around that time. Titus Vespasian crucified so many Jews in A.D. 70 that the soldiers had no room for the crosses and not enough crosses for the bodies. It wasn't until 337, when Constantine abolished crucifixion, that it disappeared after a millennium of cruelty in the world.

Crucifixion was a repugnant, demeaning form of execution for the rabble of society. The idea that anybody who died on the cross was in any sense an exceptional, elevated, noble, important person was absurd. Roman citizens generally were exempt from crucifixion unless they committed treason. The authorities reserved the cross for rebellious slaves and conquered people, and for notorious robbers and assassins. The Roman Empire's policies on crucifixion led Romans to view any crucified person as absolutely contemptible. The Romans used it only for the scum, the most humiliated, the lowest of the low.

Soldiers first flogged the victims, then forced them to carry their crossbeams, the instruments of their own deaths, to the crucifixion site. Signs around their necks indicated the crimes they had committed, and they were stark naked. Then the soldiers tied or nailed them to the crossbars, hoisted them into an upright post, and suspended them there, nude. The executioners could hurry death by shattering their legs, because that left victims unable to push themselves up in order to fill their lungs with air. If no one broke the legs, the death could last for days. The final indignity was the corpse's hanging there until the scavengers ate it.

Josephus described multiple tortures and positions of crucifixion during the siege of Jerusalem, pain suffered in every possible angle and through every possible part of the body, even unmentionable parts. Gentiles also viewed anyone crucified with the utmost contempt. It was a virtual obscenity. Polite society simply didn't discuss crucifixion. Cicero wrote, "This very word 'cross' should be removed not only from the person of a Roman citizen but from his thoughts, his eyes, his ears."

And in the face of all this, Paul came, and all he ever talked about was . . . the cross! We can see something of the deep disrespect the Gentiles had for anybody crucified in some of the pagan statements people made about Christ. Graffiti scratched on a stone in a guardroom on Palatine Hill, near Circus Maximus in Rome, shows the figure of a man with the head of an ass hanging on a cross. Below is a man in a gesture of adoration and the inscription says, "Elexa Manos worships his God." Such a repulsive depiction of the Lord Jesus Christ vividly illustrates pagan disgust for anybody crucified, and particularly a crucified God. Justin's first apology in A.D. 152 summarized the Gentile view: "They proclaim our madness to consist in this, that we give to a crucified man a place equal to the unchangeable eternal God." Nonsense!

If the Gentile attitude was bad, the Jewish attitude was worse and even more hostile. They detested the Roman practice and scorned it more than the Romans did. In their view, anybody who ever ended up on a cross fulfilled Deuteronomy 21:23, "His body shall not remain overnight on the tree . . . for he who is hanged is accursed of God." Does that mean the eternal God of Abraham, Isaac, and Jacob, the Lord Himself was cursed? How could God curse God? It's absolutely unthinkable. The Messiah cursed by God? To the Jews it was impossible to imagine.

They saw crucifixion not only as a social stigma but as a divine curse. So the stigma of the cross went beyond social disgrace, all the way to divine condemnation. The Mishnah, a second-century A.D. commentary on the law of the Pentateuch, indicated that blasphemers and idolaters alone were to be crucified; even so, the executioners hung their bodies on the cross only after they were already dead. How could the Messiah be a blasphemer? How could God be a blasphemer of God? The Jews gagged on the idea of a crucified Christ. It made the gospel unbelievable.

You think you've got problems getting the gospel across today? Imagine the early Christians. If they told the truth, they faced a massive obstacle: their claims were insane, scandalous, scurrilous, blasphemous, unbelievable.

Paul was not an easy-believism preacher. God Himself, in the form of the crucified Christ, was the biggest obstacle to believing in God. And frankly, it doesn't seem that God could have put a more formidable barrier to faith in the first century. I can't think of a worse way to market the gospel than to preach that.

The Gentiles called the Christian gospel a perverse and extravagant superstition and a sick delusion. Martin Hengel, in his instructive book *Crucifixion,* says

> To believe that the one preexistent Son of the one true God, the mediator at creation and the redeemer of the world, had appeared in very recent times in out-of-the-way Galilee as a member of the obscure people of the Jews, and even worse, had died the death of a common criminal on the cross, could only be regarded as a sign of madness. The real gods of Greece and Rome could be distinguished from mortal men by the very fact that they were *immortal*—they had absolutely nothing in common with the cross as a sign of shame . . . and thus of the one who . . . was "bound in the most ignominious fashion" and "executed in a shameful way."[3]

No wonder the Gentiles and Jews alike hated Paul's message! It was a message that was beyond human belief. No seeker-friendly message, it was either an absurdity or an obscenity.

## WISDOM MADE FOOLISH

If it wasn't enough that crucifixion bore such a shameful stigma, there was also the shameful simplicity of the cross, a repudiation of worldly wisdom. First Corinthians 1:19–21 reads:

> For it is written:
>
> > "I will destroy the wisdom of the wise,
> > And bring nothing to the understanding of the prudent."
>
> Where is the wise? Where is the scribe? Where is the disputer of this age? Has not God made foolish the wisdom of this world? For since, in the wisdom of God, the world through wisdom did not know God, it pleased God through the foolishness of the message preached to save those who believe.

Both Jew and Gentile enjoyed complexities, especially the Greeks with their philosophical systems. They loved mental gymnastics and intellectual labyrinths. They believed the truth was knowable, but only to those with elevated minds. This system later became known as gnosticism, a belief that certain people, by virtue of their enhanced reasoning powers, could move beyond the hoi polloi and ascend to the level of enlightenment.

At the time of Paul, we can trace at least fifty different philosophies rattling around in the Roman and Greek world. And the gospel came along and said, "None of it matters. We'll destroy it all. Take all the wisdom of the wise, get the best, get the elite, the most educated, the most capable, the smartest, the most clever, the best at rhetoric, oratory, logic; get all the wise, all the scribes, the legal experts, the great debaters, and they're all going to be designated fools." The gospel says they are all foolish.

Paul's quotation of Isaiah 29:14 in verse 19, "I will destroy the wisdom of the wise," had to be an offensive statement to his audience. He was basically saying, "I'll trash all you philosophers and all your philosophy." Nothing was subtle about Paul, nothing vague or ambiguous. But the message wasn't Paul's, as he reminded us when he affirmed, "It is written"—literally, "It stands written"—it stands as divinely revealed truth that the gospel of the cross makes no concession to human wisdom. Paul was just God's mouthpiece. Human intellect plays no role in redemption. And in verse 20, it's as if Paul was saying, "What do you think you have to offer? Where is the scribe? What contribution does this legal expert make? Where is the debater? What does he have to offer? They're all fools."

First Corinthians 2:14 reads, "But the natural man does not receive the things of the Spirit of God, for they are foolishness to him; nor can he know them, because they are spiritually discerned." This is the problem. An unconverted person may have great reasoning power and intellect, but when it comes to spiritual reality and the life of God and eternity, he makes no contribution. Whether it's Athens or Rome, whether it's Cambridge, Oxford, Harvard, Stanford, Yale, or Princeton, or wherever else, all the collected wisdom that is outside the Scripture adds up to nothing but foolishness.

God wisely established that no one could ever come to know Him by human wisdom. The only way anyone will come to know God is by divine revelation and through the Holy Spirit. The final word on human wisdom is that it's all nonsense. Man, by wisdom, cannot know God.

## A SCANDALOUS MESSAGE

Well, how then can man know God if not by wisdom? "Through the foolishness of the message preached." You want people to know God? Then just preach the message. Jeremiah 8:9 says, "The wise men are ashamed, / They are dismayed and taken. / Behold, they have rejected the word of the LORD; / So what wisdom do they have?" If you reject the Scripture, you don't have any wisdom. If you change the message of Scripture, you can't preach wisdom.

We have no artistic license in delivering the gospel. Look again at 1 Corinthians 1:18: "For the message of the cross is foolishness to those who are perishing, but to us who are being saved it is the power of God." Then verse 21: it is "through the foolishness of the message preached to save those who believe." And verses 23–24: "We preach Christ crucified, to the Jews a stumbling block and to the Greeks foolishness, but to those who are called, both Jews and Greeks, Christ the power of God and the wisdom of God."

Paul was giving only one message: the power of God through the word of the cross is what saves people. Men are the tools for delivering that message, but the message doesn't come from them, it comes from God. And this is absolutely the only message we have.

Any *other* message is false and absolutely unacceptable, as Galatians 1:8–9 declares without apology or compromise: "But even if we, or an angel from heaven, preach any other gospel to you than what we have preached to you, let him be accursed. As we have said before, so now I say again, if anyone preaches any other gospel to you than what you have received, let him be accursed." But the Christianity Lite that is so popular today has substituted another message that tries to eliminate the offense of the cross.

Almost no one tolerates the exclusivity and supremacy of Christ these days, even some who profess to be Christians. The message of the cross is not politically correct—it's the singularity of the gospel, on top of everything else, that bothers people. Can you imagine for a moment what might happen if a celebrity or political leader just said, "I'm a Christian and if you're not, you're going to hell"? Yikes! And then imagine if he said, "All the Muslims, Hindus, Buddhists, and all the people who believe they can earn salvation, whether liberal Protestants or Roman Catholics, and all the Mormons and Jehovah's Witnesses—you're all going to eternal hell. But I care about you so much, I want to give you the gospel of Jesus Christ, because it is far more important than wars in the Middle East, terrorism, or any domestic policy."

You can't be faithful *and* popular, so take your pick.

What Paul was saying in 1 Corinthians was that the gospel collides with our emotions; it collides with our minds; it collides with our relationships. It smashes into our sensibilities, our rational thinking, and our tolerances. It's hard to believe. And unfortunately, this is why people compromise; and when they do that, they become useless because God saves through this truth.

The cross in itself proclaims a verdict on fallen man. The cross says that God requires death for sin, while it proclaims to us the glory of substitution. It rescues the perishing. The perishing are the damned, the doomed, the ruined, the destroyed; they are the lost, under the judgment of God for endless violations of His holy law. And if you and I don't embrace the substitute, then we bear that death ourselves, and that is a death that lasts forever.

The message of the cross is not about felt needs. It is not about Jesus loving you so much He wants to make you happy. It is about rescuing you from damnation, because that is the sentence that rests upon the head of every human being. And so the gospel is an offense every way you look at it. There's nothing about the cross that fits in comfortably with how man views himself.

The gospel confronts man and exposes him for what he really is. It ignores the disappointment that he feels. It offers him no relief from the struggles of being human. Rather it goes to the profound and eternal issue of the fact that he is damned and desperately needs to be rescued. Only death can accomplish rescue, but God, in His mercy, has provided a Substitute.

## THE DREADFUL DOCTRINE

One more thing that stands in the middle of the road of easy-believism is the truth of the sovereignty of God. Years ago, I used to hear people say, "Don't ever preach the doctrine of the sovereignty of God when you have nonbelievers in the audience." People literally warned me against that. But here is another offensive bit of news for the unbeliever: God is sovereign, and you are not. You are not the captain of your soul or the master of your fate. You do not hold your destiny in your own hand.

According to 1 Corinthians 1:24, those who believe are those whom God calls and sovereignly draws. God calls them because He has *chosen* them (v. 27), *eklegomi*, picked them out for Himself. The word appears again in verse 28.

How could anybody get saved under those terms? You've got nothing left! You're absolutely stripped of everything. Verse 30: "But of Him you are in Christ Jesus, who became for us wisdom from God—and righteousness and sanctification and redemption." So, if it's all God's doing anyway, why would I tamper with the message? Why would I try to manipulate the results? Verse 31: "He who glories, let him glory in the LORD."

My friend R. C. Sproul has said that "God's favorite doctrine is sovereignty, and if you were God, it would be yours too." A wonderful sentiment like that helps offset the sick feeling I get when I hear contemporary evangelicals attack the sovereignty of God. His elective purpose is salvation, because if God isn't saving people, they won't be saved. This is a hard truth that many prominent evangelicals deny, stealing glory from God and overestimating the ability of the spiritually dead!

One very famous evangelical says: "To suggest that the merciful, long-suffering, gracious, and loving God of the Bible would invent a dreadful doctrine like election, which would have us believe it is an act of grace to select only certain people for heaven, comes perilously close to blasphemy." In other words, the claim that God sovereignly saves people by His power is almost insulting to His character. (He doesn't suggest how else they might get saved.)

Another writer, the head of a national ministry, insists, "The flawed theology of pre-selection is an attempt to eliminate man's capacity to exercise his free will, which reduces God's sovereign love to an act of a mere dictator."

Another writer believes: "Election makes our heavenly Father look like the worst of despots." Another adds that the doctrine of election is "the most unreasonable, incongruous, self-contradictory, man-belittling, God-dishonoring scheme of theology that ever appeared in Christian thought. No one can accept its contradictory, mutually exclusive propositions without intellectual self-debasement. It holds up a self-centered, selfish, heartless, remorseless tyrant for God and bids us to worship Him."

Still another says, "It makes God a monster who eternally tortures the innocent, removes the hope of consolation from the gospel, limits the atoning work of Christ, resists evangelism, stirs up argumentation and division, promotes a small, angry, judgmental God."

Here's one of the scariest of all: "To say that God sovereignly chooses is the most twisted thing I have ever read, making God into a monster, no better than a pagan idol."

What a skewed understanding of the doctrine of sovereignty! And it's based on a deficient view of sin and an unduly elevated view of fallen sinners. The fact is, according to Scripture, if God did not sovereignly open the eyes of the spiritually blind, no one would ever see. If God did not sovereignly draw sinners to Christ, none would ever come, as Romans 8:7–8 says, "because the carnal mind is enmity against God; for it is not subject to the law of God, nor indeed can be. So then, those who are in the flesh cannot please God." Nothing about this message is attractive. Believing in this doctrine is fraught with shame; it's unreasonable, illogical; and it assaults everything that is human about us, everything we love about our fallenness.

What are we left to do with this impossibility? Paul relayed the answer in 1 Corinthians 2:1–5:

> And I, brethren, when I came to you, did not come with excellence of speech or of wisdom declaring to you the testimony of God. For I determined not to know anything among you except Jesus Christ and Him crucified. I was with you in weakness, in fear, and in much trembling. And my speech and my preaching were not with persuasive words of human wisdom, but in demonstration of the Spirit and of power, that your faith should not be in the wisdom of men but in the power of God.

That's where Paul landed. He didn't shy away from the hard truth of the cross but embraced it instead, saying in effect, "I'm not looking for a popular position from which to proclaim this message or advance it on the back of public favor. I preach the shameful cross because that's what I've been told to preach. And I leave it to the sovereign power of God to work through that message to produce a faith that rests not on the wisdom of men, but on the power of God." Would that we can say the same.

# 3

## TRUTH IN A PRIVY POT

Christians, it would seem, are stuck with a very unattractive product to promote: Christ on the cross. This is a weak, shameful image that offends the sensibilities and shocks the refined emotions of decent people. The claim that Roman soldiers executed the God of the universe on a cross, like a criminal, also assaults our rational minds. It's an affront to the pride we carry for having the gift of reason that puts us above the animals.

Plenty of tolerant people out there say, "Okay, you're into this cross thing, and Jesus being crucified, and that's your truth. Good for you—we are an inclusive people. You're welcome to your foolish view of religion, your foolish perspective, your simple, silly story of a crucified Jew, and that's fine if that's your truth. But that's not our truth."

Well, here's the rub: It *is* your truth. It's *everybody's* truth. It's the *only* truth. The power of the crucified Christ is the only power of God by which He saves. Salvation comes only through a belief in that gospel, the gospel of Jesus. No gospel, no salvation. The absolute exclusivity of it has always been a shameful, embarrassing, inconvenient message to worldly-wise sinners, but the truth is nonnegotiable. Other religions are not truth and lead only to eternal damnation. Islam is a damning system. Buddhism is a damning system. Hinduism is a damning system. Simply not believing the gospel is itself enough to damn a person.

People in false religions do not worship the true God by another name, as some suggest. They unwittingly worship Satan's demons. Here is what the Bible says: "The things which the Gentiles sacrifice they sacrifice to demons and not to God" (1 Cor. 10:20). Even so, a book called *The Christ of Hinduism* actually exists, and it argues that Hinduism's symbols and doctrines contain the Christian message. But there is no Christ of Hinduism, nor has the true God any part in Hinduism. Christ is the only way to the one true God, and biblical Christianity is the only way to the one true Christ. Misguided people who recognize any other god and engage in any other religion are not worshipping and sacrificing to God, but to demons. I didn't make this up. This isn't my theology. This is Christianity 101.

## VIPs WANTED

The true, exclusive, narrow gospel is hard enough to believe as it is. But to make things worse, from the start those promoting it were rejected people who had no standing or respect in society, like Paul, who preached this foolish message faithfully. The people proclaiming the most important and hard-to-believe truth are generally the ones the world despises, belittles, and ignores.

In A.D. 178, Celsus wrote that Christians were the most vulgar and uneducated people around. No wonder. In 1 Corinthians 1:26–29, Paul told us that was by divine design. God has purposely chosen the foolish, the nonintellectuals to shame the wise:

> For you see your calling, brethren, that not many wise according
> to the flesh, not many mighty, not many noble, are called. But
> God has chosen the foolish things of the world to put to shame
> the wise, and God has chosen the weak things of the world to put

to shame the things which are mighty; and the base things of the world and the things which are despised God has chosen, and the things which are not, to bring to nothing the things that are, that no flesh should glory in His presence.

God has chosen the weak—Paul's word in verse 27 is *asthenes*, void of strength, void of power. He has chosen the base—*agenes*, people of no birth, without any significance. This characterization of Christians as intellectual lowbrows is embedded in popular culture today. Many powerful people would agree with billionaire media mogul Ted Turner when he said, "Christianity is for losers." As Paul reminded us so many times, God's way is different from the world's, and His definition of winning has nothing to do with boardroom politics or the size of your bank account. The prize here is eternal life.

I read a story years ago that claimed to be about the most insignificant person ever born. His mother wrote his name on the birth certificate as Nosmo King. Somebody asked the mother where she got a name like that. It turned out the mother was illiterate, so she just copied down the No Smoking sign in the room and wrote it "Nosmo King." There is the ultimate nothing person, named after a No Smoking sign.

If you speak the hard gospel of Jesus Christ, you may be pegged as one of the Nosmo Kings of the world: a loser, a nobody. Verse 28 of 1 Corinthians 1 says God has chosen things that are "despised," *exoutheneo*, considered nothing. Christians are about as low as you can go. We are "the things which are not," literally "the nonexistent ones." It's human nature to want to *be somebody*. So the Lord decided to do it a different way, choosing as His messengers the impotent, nonintellectual nobodies whom the world considers nothing by its standards.

Don't you wonder what in the world God was thinking here? Wouldn't He want to choose VIPs? Wouldn't He want *somebodies* on His team? He's the Creator—He can have anybody He wants. We have enough to get over with just the message and the invitation. Wouldn't it help if some really important people were working on this?

Considering that the message is so unattractive and hard to believe, maybe what we need is really great messengers. We need some world-class intellectuals, some royalty, some beautiful people, some celebrities, some big-league sports stars who will make all this embarrassing, confrontational stuff go down easier. Perhaps we can overcome consumer resistance if we get some people in lofty places, the high and the mighty, the powerful and the influential; then, even though the message is totally bizarre nonsense, maybe they could sell it.

I've heard this proposal often through the years. If only some famous person could get saved, just think about the power his testimony would have! Or if this famous athlete or personality in the media, the arts, or politics could only be a Christian, just imagine the impact of his testimony. But it doesn't work that way. No matter how powerful and influential some preachers of the gospel become within the culture, posturing from positions of prestige can't compensate for the distastefulness of the message or overcome the stubbornness of the sinner's will. Besides, what recording artist or movie star is going to be willing to stand up at the Grammys or the Oscars and share the gospel? The audience would boo him off the stage. He can thank Jesus for winning, but pandemonium would ensue if he proclaimed the truths of hell, sin, repentance, and salvation only in Jesus Christ.

Nevertheless, it seems like a good idea. And while God, in His wisdom, might send us a movie star with his heart on fire for the gospel, it's not likely, according to Paul. Look at his language in verse 26: "For you see your calling, brethren, that not many wise . . ."—*sophos*, not many intellectuals, not many mighty, not many wielding power, not many nobles or aristocrats.

I don't mean to say that only unsuccessful, unknown people in the world are Christians and willing to share the whole truth of Jesus' teaching. A few popular folks are believers, and occasionally you'll run into one. Living near Los Angeles, I sometimes encounter stars and known personalities, and at times, evidence that the Holy Spirit is at work on them has encouraged me.

Once after Larry King interviewed me, I got a call from a very prominent entertainment figure, who said, "I've got to talk to you." I went to his house in Beverly Hills and spent two hours listening to his religious beliefs and explaining the authority of Scripture and the exclusivity of Christ to him. Apparently, out of everything that I and others on the show said, it was biblical authority and Jesus Christ as the only Savior that disturbed him. He was searching; he was interested—but the narrowness of the gospel was more than he could accept. I hope someday, when all his other options for heart peace have proven empty, that the seed of the gospel will flourish in him.

Few experiences in my life have been more wonderful than watching the spiritual journey of one of the greatest classical guitarists of our time, Christopher Parkening. Chris grew up in southern California and had a record contract with a top international label before he was twenty. Within a few years he was a worldwide star. His goal was to be a millionaire by the time he was thirty, and he made it with time to spare. He booked concerts years in advance, and his records were bestsellers in the U.S. and Europe.

But like the ant who struggles to the top of the anthill only to realize there's nothing to see, Chris achieved all his goals yet had no contentment or fulfillment in his life. One day, in God's providence, he heard about our church from a neighbor and decided to give it a try. His soul opened to the strong influence of the Holy Spirit and he bowed to the lordship of Jesus Christ. Today he's not only a dear friend, but a faithful follower of our Lord, joyfully submissive to the Word of God. And the love of Christ enriches and completes his life in a way no amount of earthly success could. He's become a classical music ambassador for the Lord. At his concerts, he gives away recordings of his testimony; the fame that once served only for material gain now gives Chris the privilege of proclaiming his sovereign Savior to thousands who might never otherwise hear the true gospel.

Once in a while, the grace of God converts prominent people. Even so, the gospel has never moved through history, filling the redemptive plan, by relying on the prestige of influential personalities. It moves, for the most part, with us—the unimpressive, impotent, nothing, nobodies.

## BAKED DIRT

Why does God do this? He does it to shame the wise, to shame the strong, to nullify them. God doesn't want smart, powerful people to receive credit for what He alone does. Paul used a form of *katargeo* in 1 Corinthians 1:28, meaning "to neutralize them, to render them inoperative." God renders all their great earthly intellect inoperative. He takes the gospel away from the world's somebodies and gives it to the nobodies, so that in the end, verse 29, "no flesh should glory in His presence": no person can take credit for the advancement of the gospel. No human will ever take credit for this divine work.

Paul made this even more clear in 2 Corinthians 4:5–7, when he wrote, "For we do not preach ourselves, but Christ Jesus the Lord, and ourselves your bondservants for Jesus' sake. For it is the God who commanded light to shine out of darkness, who has shone in our hearts to give the light of the knowledge of the glory of God in the face of Jesus Christ. But we have this treasure in earthen vessels, that the excellence of the power may be of God and not of us."

Paul called those who carry and preach the treasure of the true gospel *ostrakinos*, translated here as "earthen vessels." "Earthen vessel" is frankly too dignified a term; not that it's very dignified, but it's too dignified to translate the word *ostrakinos*. This is a cheap baked clay pot, unrefined, ugly, breakable, replaceable, valueless. It's the little pot in which you put your plants.

The contrast is staggering. We have this treasure of the glorious light of the gospel, the one shining in our hearts, the light of the knowledge of the glory of God in the face of Christ, in us—in cheap earthenware.

Paul was picking up all the brilliance, all the glory of the true revelation of God's nature manifest in Christ. He was trying to describe what is most indescribably and inexplicably beautiful in saying this treasure—the treasure of the divine reality of the gospel—resided in clay pots! We're baked dirt, that's what we are, carrying around the message of God's eternal kingdom of light and life.

People scorned Paul for his unimpressive image. His critics said that his presence was unattractive, and his speech was absolutely "contemptible" (2 Cor. 10:10). He had a bodily condition that was repulsive. Some scholars think he had some terrible stuff oozing out of his eyes. He did not have "the look" you need to be popular and successful today. No stage presence whatsoever. He demonstrated no oratorical skill, intellectual acumen, or sophistication like the popular, charming philosophers and rabbis of his day. He was just baked clay. But that was okay with him, because that was the way God had designed it, and that made it very evident what the power's source was. And did that power ever flow through him!

I've read and reread *William Tyndale*, David Daniells's substantial biography. Thomas More was a great defender of Roman Catholicism in England, and he felt himself the servant of God in taking on William Tyndale and doing everything he could to destroy his work. Tyndale did what More thought was an absolutely horrible thing: he translated the Bible into a language people could read, in defiance of the Catholic hierarchy of the time. They were afraid the church would lose its influence if any common person off the street, and not just the official interpreters of the church who knew Latin, could read and understand the Bible. Tyndale's contemporaries relentlessly persecuted Tyndale, forcing him to live in exile with the knowledge that if he went back to England, his enemies would kill him, as they were killing the people who read his New Testament. Eventually they hunted him down, then imprisoned and executed him in France. His crime? Translating the Bible into English.

Thomas More attacked not only William Tyndale but Martin Luther as well. Part of Tyndale's condemnation was that he was a follower of Luther. More came up with a clever little title for Luther: he called him "a privy pot." Do I need to exegete that? He was the pot that human waste went into in the days before modern plumbing. Thomas More used a scatological insult to try to demean Luther (and Martin was not averse to replying to his critics with some scatology of his own). Regrettably, such language was used even in some of the theological debates of that time.

But More was close to being right. He meant it as an insult, but in fact it proves he was only echoing what Scripture says. In 2 Timothy 2:20, Paul wrote: "But in a great house there are not only vessels of gold and silver, but also of wood and clay, some for honor and some for dishonor." You have some containers in a large house that are gold and silver. But you also have other containers that are wooden buckets and clay pots. And the ones that are gold and silver have honorable purposes, and the ones that are wood and clay have dishonorable purposes. Now just use your imagination. Food came in on the gold and silver, and it went out on the earth and wood.

Paul knew what he was talking about when he called Christians "earthen vessels." We're baked clay. We're privy pots. The advance of the gospel will never occur on account of us.

This helps explain why God chose none of the early preachers among the apostles because of his superior intellect, position, or prominence. As I wrote in my book *Twelve Ordinary Men*, these twelve were so ordinary it defies all human logic: not one teacher, not one priest, not one rabbi, not one scribe, not one Pharisee, not one Sadducee, not even a synagogue ruler—nobody from the elite. Half of them or so were fishermen, and the rest were common laborers. One, Simon the Zealot, was a terrorist, a member of a group who went around with daggers in their cloaks, trying to stab Romans. Then there was Judas, the loser of all losers.

What was the Lord doing? He picked people with absolutely no influence. None of the great intellects from Egypt, Greece, Rome, or Israel was among the apostles. During the New Testament time, the greatest scholars were very likely in Egypt. The most distinguished philosophers were in Athens. The powerful were in Rome. The biblical scholars were in Jerusalem. God disdained all of them and picked clay pots instead. Think of it like this: He passed by Herodotus, the historian; He passed by Socrates, the great thinker. He passed by the father of medicine, Hippocrates. He passed by Plato the philosopher, Aristotle the wise, Euclid the mathematician, Archimedes the father of mechanics, Hipparchus the astronomer, Cicero the orator, and Virgil the poet. He didn't pay attention to any of those people when selecting the preachers of the difficult-to-believe message of salvation.

He's still doing it. He is still in the business of passing up the gold and silver bowls and picking up clay pots.

## THE SCUM

Do you think your self-esteem has taken a pounding so far? There's more to come. In 1 Corinthians 4:6, Paul wrote: "Now these things, brethren, I have figuratively transferred to myself and Apollos for your sakes, that you may learn in us not to think beyond what is written, that none of you may be puffed up on behalf of one against the other." He had been talking about the fact that he didn't want anybody to consider him anything: "Let a man so consider us, as servants of Christ and stewards of the mysteries of God" (v. 1). In other words, "Don't make anything out of me. Don't name cathedrals or cities in Minnesota in my honor. I'm just a servant of Christ, a steward of the mysteries of God. I'm an under-rower, a third-level galley slave; I pull my oar, and that's what I'm supposed to do, nothing worthy of special attention."

In verse 3 he said it didn't matter what we thought about him: "It is a very small thing that I should be judged by you or by a human court. In fact, I do not even judge myself." He was saying, "I don't even care what I say about myself. You don't know the truth, and I'm biased in my favor, and neither one of us is likely to be accurate. Don't pass judgment. Let the Lord do that. We can't be thinking about each other in terms of who's more important than the next person. We're all just clay pots."

First Corinthians 4:7: "For who makes you differ from another? And what do you have that you did not receive? Now if you did indeed receive it, why do you boast as if you had not received it?" He was starting to get a little sarcastic. Verse 8: "You are already full! You are already rich! You have reigned as kings without us— and indeed I could wish you did reign, that we also might reign with you!"

And then Paul made this amazing statement in verse 9: "For I think that God has displayed us, the apostles, last, as men condemned to death; for we have been made a spectacle to the world, both to angels and to men." Paul considered the apostles the lowest of the low, like criminals on death row whom their captors dragged through the streets on the way to their executions.

In verse 13, he said, "We have been made as the filth of the world, the offscouring of all things until now." Another way to translate it is, "We have become the scum of the world and the dregs of all things." Scum? Dregs? This is hardly any way to attract a crowd of followers. *Perikatharma* is the word for scum. *Katharma*, related to "catharsis," is "to cleanse," and *peri* is the word for encircling or around. The *perikatharma* is the scum that stays in the bottom of the pot, the residue someone has to scrub thoroughly to remove. People in the ancient world used the word metaphorically to describe the lowest class of criminals that officials offered as human sacrifices to appease the false deities they feared. If you wanted to get your angry god off your back, because you thought he sent a famine or a plague or you lost a war, you found some scum in your society, some filthy nobody that no one would miss and you wanted eliminated anyway, and you put him on an altar as a sacrifice to appease your deity. Paul said that is how the world sees us. We're the scum.

Then he said we are the *peripsema*, the dregs. We just keep falling lower here. You could remove the *perikatharma* by cleaning thoroughly. This stuff is the caked crud that won't come off until you scrape it off. It is the last, stubborn, utterly useless refuse to cling to the bottom of a pot that you had emptied and cleansed.

Are you beginning to get an idea of the hopelessness of this task? The invitation to salvation makes people literally kill off all their dreams, ambitions, felt needs, and selfish desires. And then we call them to a repentance and faith that is absolutely against the grain of every normal human impulse. To compound our problem, the vast majority of the people who are offering this are scum in the eyes of the world.

If I were devising a plan to make an impact on fallen humanity, this would not be my approach: come up with an impossible message, an impossible invitation, and then market it with the most unimpressive people in the world, the ones others will most likely belittle and demean, if not hate and vilify—and sometimes kill.

## PAUL'S GOSPEL STRATEGY

The message is shameful, and the messengers are privy pots. This situation seems absolutely hopeless. What possible strategy can rescue Christians and the gospel from such miserable, impossible circumstances? How can they possibly survive?

Paul gave us the answers with confidence in 2 Corinthians 4, couched in terms of what *not* to do. First, we will not surrender in cowardice. Verse 1: "Therefore, since we have this ministry, as we have received mercy, we do not lose heart." Paul assumed people would reject him. He expected hostility. He knew hatred would meet his words. Still, saying we do not "lose heart," *enkakeomen*, literally means we don't give in to evil, we don't lose courage. We will not become fainthearted, we will not crumble under this treatment because in our crumbling, we are useless to God.

The false teachers Paul encountered in Corinth were market savvy. They were the original seeker-friendly strategists, selling their images, packaging their messages with what people wanted to hear. People wanted their religion a little metaphysical, a little oratorical, a little philosophical, a little transcendental, a little allegorical, and a little legalistic. And they wanted it in the mouths of the slick. Those who took this approach avoided the hostility the true preachers received. Paul knew better than to cater to those demands. He said, "I will not be a coward. We will not lose heart." He refused to feel discouraged and compromise the truth just because it could cost him big!

Strategy point number two: We will not tamper with the message. Verse 2: "We have renounced the hidden things of shame, not walking in craftiness or handling the word of God deceitfully, but by manifestation of truth commending ourselves to every man's conscience in the sight of God." It is tough; it is impossible; it is hard; it is painful; but we will not become cowards, and we will not tamper with the truth. We will not walk in *panourgia*, in trickery, adulterating the Word of God, tampering with the gospel to make it less offensive, in order for men to commend us. Instead, we will be faithful to the gospel, manifesting the truth in order to commend ourselves to every man's conscience, with God watching. We will not surrender. We will not alter the message.

Third, we will not manipulate people to get the desired superficial results, because we know, as 2 Corinthians 4:3–4 affirms, that "even if our gospel is veiled, it is veiled to those who are perishing, whose minds the god of this age has blinded, who do not believe, lest the light of the gospel of the glory of Christ, who is the image of God, should shine on them." The problem is not the seed, it's the soil. It's the unreceptive, barren condition of the human heart. Paul said he would not use words and techniques that manipulated the results, because he understood that when people don't believe, it is because they are in the condition of spiritual deadness. They are perishing and blind, thanks to Satan. If our gospel is veiled to someone, it is veiled because that person, like all sinners, is unable to understand. Changing the message, manipulating the emotions or the will, is useless, since no one can believe unless God grants him understanding.

Nothing is wrong with the message. Nothing can be. It is God's Word! How could we be so brash as to change it? If they don't hear the truth, cool music won't help. If they don't see the light, PowerPoint won't help. If they don't like the message, drama and video won't help. They're blind and dead. Our task is to go on preaching not ourselves, not our manipulated message, but repentance and submission to Christ Jesus as Lord. The message never changes. We may be nothing more than baked dirt, but we carry a supernatural message of everlasting life that we will not surrender.

Paul's fourth strategic point is that we will not seek popularity.
Verses 8–12:

> We are hard-pressed on every side, yet not crushed; we are per-
> plexed, but not in despair; persecuted, but not forsaken; struck
> down, but not destroyed—always carrying about in the body the
> dying of the Lord Jesus, that the life of Jesus also may be mani-
> fested in our body. For we who live are always delivered to death
> for Jesus' sake, that the life of Jesus also may be manifested in our
> mortal flesh. So then death is working in us, but life in you.

Here's the key, in verse 13: "Since we have the same spirit of faith,
according to what is written [in Psalm 116:10], 'I believed and therefore I spoke,' we also believe and therefore speak."

We shouldn't expect popularity. What should we expect? Paul
gave us the list: affliction, crushing, persecution, being knocked flat,
and always carrying about in the body the dying of Jesus. That doesn't
describe some mystical asceticism; it simply means that He was
always on the brink of death, always ready to die, always being pur-
sued by some who were plotting death. He knew that every day He
awakened could be the day He died. Death was working in Him as
a daily experience, a constant anticipation. In His mind, He had to
live daily through His own funeral because He could die any time.
Yet this great truth never changed: "I believed and therefore I spoke."
That's it, Christian. You believe, and you speak.

Strategic point number five: We will not look at earthly success.
Why not? Because we believe and speak,

> Knowing that He who raised up the Lord Jesus will also raise us
> up with Jesus, and will present us with you. For all things are for
> your sakes, that grace, having spread through the many, may
> cause thanksgiving to abound to the glory of God. Therefore we

do not lose heart. Even though our outward man is perishing, yet the inward man is being renewed day by day. For our light affliction, which is but for a moment, is working for us a far more exceeding and eternal weight of glory, while we do not look at the things which are seen, but at the things which are not seen. For the things which are seen are temporary, but the things which are not seen are eternal. (2 Cor. 4:14–16)

We're not concerned with the temporal and transient. Our success isn't measured in hours, or even centuries. Our focus is fixed on eternity.

The gospel is hard to believe, and the people who bring it to the world are nobodies. The plan is still the same for all who are God's clay pots. To summarize, here is Paul's humble, five-point strategy: We will not lose heart. We will not alter the message. We will not manipulate the results, because we understand that a profound spiritual reality is at work in those who do not believe. We will not expect popularity, and therefore, we will not be disappointed. And we will not be concerned with visible and earthly success but devote our efforts toward that which is unseen and eternal.

In 2 Corinthians 4:6–7, Paul wrote, "For it is the God who commanded light to shine out of darkness, who has shone in our hearts to give the light of the knowledge of the glory of God in the face of Jesus Christ. But we have this treasure in earthen vessels, that the excellence of the power may be of God and not of us." And that brings us full circle to where we started in this chapter: at the end of the day there is no human explanation for the growth of the church. The world thinks we're odd and bizarre. We're the losers. We're the privy pots. And yet, through the mouths of Paul and other misfits across the centuries, the church inexplicably moves in the history of the world with immense power beyond anything else. The gospel alone turns sinners into saints by transplanting men and women from the kingdom of darkness into the kingdom of God's dear Son—from eternal death to everlasting life. That is power to create new beings fit for God's presence and glory.

If we brought a bus load of movie stars, corporate titans, or Ivy League professors into our church (assuming they'd condescend to get on a bus), they'd look at us and laugh: "These people can't change the world!" No, we can't. But for those who remain faithful to the whole truth of Christianity, God is changing the world through us. He's been doing it through all history.

# 4

## THE BEST EXAMPLE

Paul suffered and struggled mightily in the service of his faith. Perhaps you could argue that he simply wasn't the best example after which to model our own behavior. What if we look at the ultimate example of a Christian teacher and expositor, Christ Himself? Surely then we'll see how to handle this unappealing message of a crucified Savior whom only the dregs of society preached. Surely at last we'll see a glimmer of success.

But by worldly standards, when Jesus began preaching His own gospel in His own hometown, He was an even more spectacular failure than Paul! This episode in Jesus' life is one of the most gripping and powerful portions of the Bible. His words in Scripture capture the shock and emotion of the moment, and they still stun us with their power and their force.

The riveting drama begins in Luke 4, verses 16 through 21:

So He came to Nazareth, where He had been brought up. And as His custom was, He went into the synagogue on the Sabbath day, and stood up to read. And He was handed the book of the prophet Isaiah. And when He had opened the book, He found the place where it was written:

"The Spirit of the LORD is upon Me,
Because He anointed Me
To preach the gospel to the poor;
He has sent Me to heal the brokenhearted,
To proclaim liberty to the captives
And recovery of sight to the blind,
To set at liberty those who are oppressed;
To proclaim the acceptable year of the LORD."

Then He closed the book, and gave it back to the attendant and sat down. And the eyes of all who were in the synagogue were fixed on Him. And He began to say to them, "Today this Scripture is fulfilled in your hearing."

Imagine going to church next Sunday, expecting to hear your pastor preaching, and having the Lord Jesus Christ appear in person to tell you that He had come to fulfill all the prophecies of His second coming—all the prophecies of the glory of His kingdom of salvation on earth! Imagine that you had gone that morning, and Jesus was standing in the pulpit to tell you that the time was now for the fulfillment of all divine promises connected to His return.

Well, that's something like what the Jews in the Nazareth synagogue experienced that day. They had attended that synagogue all their lives, and they had heard reading after reading of the Torah, the Law, and the Haftarah, the prophets, and sermon after sermon on Sabbath after Sabbath throughout their lifetimes. They had heard much teaching about the Messiah, and they had been reading many Scriptures about His coming and kingdom. But all of a sudden, on this Sabbath in the year A.D. 28, in an obscure synagogue in a nothing blue-collar town called Nazareth, He was there!

All those many years, they had gathered to hear the Law and the prophets, and the Law and the prophets had all spoken of the Messiah. They had attended a local synagogue, which Philo described as a house of instruction where the people heard the Scripture read and explained. Many, many times the text was messianic, and as they listened, their hearts filled with the hope of the Messiah's arrival. Their history had been bleak for centuries. The pagan Romans were their masters, and hope in the Messiah was often dim. But on this day the Messiah arrived and was Himself the reader and the expositor of the Scripture.

The reputation of Jesus as a teacher and miracle-worker had been growing, and that's why they were so excited that He was going to speak in His own hometown. Verses 14 and 15 tell us, "News of Him went out through all the surrounding region. And He taught in their synagogues, being glorified by all." His reputation was gathering by the time He entered this synagogue in Nazareth to launch His year-and-a-half Galilean ministry. He had already been ministering almost a year in the south, in Judea, with a few visits to Galilee. So by this time, the word was spreading about Him.

He went to His own boyhood synagogue. If, as historians tell us, the town of Nazareth had about twenty thousand people, it would have had several synagogues. They were scattered throughout the neighborhoods the way local churches were in days when everyone walked to church, and this was His family's local synagogue. All the familiar faces were there. He would have walked into that synagogue and seen the neighbors He grew up with, as well as a host of aunts, uncles, cousins, and other relatives.

So far the story of Jesus' ministry had been pretty positive. All the way through the four chapters of Luke's gospel, and for more than a year of His ministry, everything had gone well. And here, at the beginning of this meeting in his hometown synagogue, we learn that He was "glorified by all."

## PHYSICIAN, HEAL YOURSELF!

But very shortly, things took a nasty turn. Continuing in Luke 4:22–30:

> So all bore witness to Him, and marveled at the gracious words which proceeded out of His mouth. And they said, "Is this not Joseph's son?" He said to them, "You will surely say this proverb to Me, 'Physician, heal yourself!' Whatever we have heard done in Capernaum [possibly some healing miracles], do also here in Your country." Then He said, "Assuredly, I say to you, no prophet is accepted in his own country. But I tell you truly, many widows were in Israel in the days of Elijah, when the heaven was shut up three years and six months, and there was a great famine throughout all the land; but to none of them was Elijah sent except to Zarephath, in the region of Sidon, to a woman who was a widow. And many lepers were in Israel in the time of Elisha the prophet, and none of them was cleansed except Naaman the Syrian."
>
> So all those in the synagogue, when they heard these things, were filled with wrath, and rose up and thrust Him out of the city; and they led Him to the brow of the hill on which their city was built, that they might throw Him down over the cliff. Then passing through the midst of them, He went His way.

This was absolutely shocking. What was happening? What went wrong? It all began so assuringly. Jesus read messianic prophecies from Isaiah 61:1–2, then a section from Isaiah 58:6, and then He explained that that day, the Scripture had been fulfilled. In other words, He told them He was the fulfillment of all messianic promises. He was saying that He was the long-awaited Messiah, right there in their midst, and they were hearing Him speak. He had come to accomplish God's ancient promises, to bring the favorable year of the Lord, which meant the era of salvation. He, the Savior who would bring the salvation, was standing in front of them, and they were listening to His voice and looking at His face. With Him came salvation to the poor, the prisoners, the blind, the outcasts, the distressed, the oppressed, and the downtrodden.

His message was unmistakable: "Salvation is available to those of you who confess your spiritual poverty, who confess your spiritual bondage, who confess your spiritual darkness, who confess your spiritual defeat." Many times the rabbi had stood up in the synagogue and said, "The blessed hour of the Messiah is to come. The people who are eyewitnesses of the Messiah Himself will be greatly blessed. The eyes honored to look at the sight of the Messiah are of all eyes most blessed, and the ears honored to hear His voice are of all ears most blessed." That day, those Jews were those eyewitnesses. They were the blessed of all nations, of all generations, because it was to them that He came, to that little group in that unimportant town in that small synagogue. To them had come the Messiah of God, the Savior of the world, with the message of salvation, of spiritual riches, of forgiveness, of deliverance and eternal life.

No Sabbath ever began so wondrously. Yet no Sabbath ever ended so tragically.

It rivets you to the page, wondering how this could have happened. How could Jesus let it turn out so badly? Wasn't He smarter than that? At first, His words settled well, and everyone marveled at them. Now, that doesn't mean they believed in Him as the Messiah, it just means that the buzz was very positive. And the reason was that they were in awe of the gracious words falling from His lips. They may have been wondering about His message. Some of them must have questioned why He stopped reading in the middle of Isaiah 61:2, where it talked about "the acceptable year of the LORD," though the rest of the verse said, "and the day of vengeance of our God."

Why did He leave the vengeance out? True, they were very eager for the Messiah's coming, but honestly, they were just as eager for Him to come and wreak vengeance on their Gentile enemies as they were for Him to come and bring salvation to Israel. They hated their oppressors. It must have bothered some of them that Jesus stopped short in His reading. Even John the Baptist had talked about the Messiah's unquenchable judgment of fire. They were more than ready for that.

But the day of vengeance was in the future. Jesus wasn't there that day for vengeance on anyone; He was there for salvation. And through His whole life, He avoided expressions of vengeance. He was on earth for the salvation of anyone and everyone who recognized that he was poor, a prisoner, blind, and oppressed.

Jesus' listeners were even more struck by His ability to communicate. Powerful orators have always been able to captivate people. Time and again throughout history, great speakers making great speeches have won over the minds and hearts of their listeners. These people had just heard the greatest speaker who ever lived. The words that fell from His lips were like words they had never heard from anyone, ever. Luke didn't record the whole sermon, but it was an explanation of those Old Testament prophecies. I'd like to think it lasted at least an hour.

The people were stunned at His ability to speak because they had never heard Him teach or preach before, even though He had grown up in their midst. And when He did, they were in awe. He was the greatest communicator who ever opened His mouth, possessing impeccable and consummate understanding of truth, pure and holy passion for that truth, flawless reasoning, accurate interpretation, and unmatched dexterity with the language. I'm sure His voice and movements were sheer perfection—as everything about Him was.

Jesus astonished them. No one would have said what the critics of Paul said: "His presence is unimpressive and his speech contemptible." Just the opposite was true. Jesus was amazing in presence and speech. And they kept repeating, "Isn't that Joseph the carpenter's son?" Then familiarity bred its normal contempt. They couldn't deny the majesty of His oratory. They couldn't hedge on the masterful way He had communicated the message. It was unlike anything they had ever heard. But what didn't fit in the picture was that this *was* Joseph the carpenter's kid, who used to run around in the neighborhood. They couldn't imagine He was the one whom God in heaven was talking about when He said, "This is My beloved Son."

They were in awe of His communication ability and stirred because they heard the truth presented in absolute perfection and wisdom. They understood exactly what He said, and the message, again, was that salvation was available for the poor, the prisoners, the blind, and the oppressed. (And those are the only ones who will be saved!) Jesus' relatives and neighbors got the message. If they wanted salvation, they had to confess their spiritual poverty, their spiritual blindness, and their spiritual bondage. They would have to deny themselves, that is, admit their spiritual destitution.

What went wrong was that the true gospel, even majestically preached in pure perfection and power, was no more of a crowd pleaser than it is today. Where's the fun and self-satisfaction in admitting you're spiritually destitute? That is the last thing the Jews were prepared to do. And Jesus never even got to the part about taking up a cross! They were righteous in their own eyes. They were noble, God's chosen and devout. They worshipped the true and living God of Israel. They went to every synagogue event. They gave their tithes. They prayed. They fasted.

They were like that Luke 18 Pharisee: they were the people of God. They were like Paul in Philippians 3: they were circumcised and they had their tribal pedigree. They were of the people of Israel. They were traditionalists. They were ceremonialists. They were zealous for the Law. They kept the Law outwardly as blamelessly as they could.

They were thinking, "Hey, we're not the spiritually poor, the prisoners, the blind, and the oppressed. That's got to be somebody else. That's got to be—*the Gentiles*! And we don't like the insinuation that we are!"

Of course, Jesus knew what their reaction would be. But did He tailor His remarks to please the crowd? Did He safeguard His reputation by telling them what they wanted to hear and what would make them comfortable? Did He ignore the truth in favor of their little felt needs? No, He told them the ragged and unadorned truth and let the chips fall where they would. In doing that He gives us the best example, the perfect example, of preaching the gospel, remaining faithful to the truth, even though His oldest friends and closest relatives tried to kill Him for it. It takes strong indictment to turn your nearest and dearest against you this fast. Yet after one sermon, they had become a lynch mob wanting to kill Jesus!

His familiar audience was engulfed in a wave of denial and self-preservation: "We can't buy this message, and the problem can't be us, so it must be Him. How do we know He's the Messiah, anyway?" So they just put up a wall, denying the obvious proofs: "We don't know that He's the Messiah." And Jesus read their minds, as He had done in the past. John 2:24–25 records that when He was in Judea, the people came to Jesus but He didn't commit Himself to them "because He knew what was in man." He was omniscient; He knew their plan. So He said to them in Luke 4:23, "You will surely say this proverb to Me, 'Physician, heal yourself! Whatever we have heard done at Capernaum, do also here in Your country.'" In other words, "If You want us to believe in You, then, Physician, heal Yourself. Don't tell us You're the doctor if You don't have some proof."

He offered them words of salvation, forgiveness, good news, release, and He also did miracles in their midst. To receive all of that, though, they had to be willing to admit they were the poor, prisoners, blind, and oppressed. That was absolutely unthinkable. No such confession was ever going to rise out of their self-righteous hearts, hard hearts filled with pride and religious conceit. And Jesus knew that because He reads hearts like an open book.

But here's a related point that's easy to overlook: miracles were completely beside the point. Even if Jesus could perform miracles, that would not have proved He could save sinners. If Jesus provided a miracle, would that have been proof that He could transfer people from the kingdom of darkness to the kingdom of light? If He produced a miracle, would that demonstrate that He could save your soul from hell? Would it verify that He could give you eternal life and take you to heaven? *No.*

You can take all the so-called miracle-workers, from Jannes, Jambres, and the Egyptian magicians all the way down to Simon Magus in the New Testament; you can take all the oracles of Delphi and all the black magicians and white magicians and bring them all together; you can take all the hocus-pocus faith healers and TV evangelists, line them up, and have them perform their whole gig of so-called miracles. Yet when they're finished, whether they're true or false, they do not prove that Jesus Christ can save someone from hell. All of this supposed miracle-working on television today has absolutely no bearing on the power of the gospel. I don't know what those "healers" think they're accomplishing by falsifying miracles— as if falsifying miracles somehow is going to cause people to believe in Jesus Christ. It isn't. It doesn't. It never did—Jesus banished disease and demons from the whole land of Israel with *authentic* miracles, and they put Him on a cross.

Miracles weren't the real issue with Jesus' audience because they couldn't legitimately question Jesus' ability to perform them. They proved that when they wanted Him to do in Nazareth what they knew He'd done twenty miles away in Capernaum. He had performed miracles there, as well as the one at the wedding in nearby Cana, when He made wine. And other miracles occurred in Judea and Galilee that must have been well-known to the Galileans, who were often there for Passover and other feasts. So the accumulated information about the miracles was growing, and the evidence was so irrefutable that they didn't question them. In other words, they believed He had done amazing signs elsewhere. Now they wanted Him to do some in front of them.

For a fact, in all the New Testament, the Jewish population and Jewish leaders never questioned the miracles of Jesus. In John 11:47, the Pharisees and chief priests admitted Jesus was "working signs," or performing miracles. They never doubted that, and so their question to Jesus was not an honest one. They were thinking, "We'd like to believe that You're the Messiah, who brings salvation and the promised kingdom, and that You can take the spiritually poor and make them rich, the spiritually bound and make them free, the spiritually blind and make them see, the spiritually oppressed and fearful and deliver them. So to prove it, could You please spin up in the air, do a cartwheel or two in space, and come back down?" That wouldn't have proved anything about salvation power.

They were like modern-day politicians who can't win on the issues, so they change the subject and attack their opponents personally, or drone on about their own pet projects without any regard to the subject at hand. The people of Nazareth were unsympathetic to His message, which was that if they wanted to have salvation, they had to see their spiritual bankruptcy and the true condition of their wicked hearts. They were too proud and too self-righteous; they were too skeptical in their carefully crafted self-defense mode.

Jesus said He was the Messiah, and the people insisted that He prove it—"Physician, heal yourself"—in a way that blunted or redirected the essence of His message. "Don't challenge our preconceptions about faith or our view of ourselves. It's not our fault that we don't believe, Jesus; it's Your fault. Your show isn't positive and convincing and entertaining."

Miracles do affirm the faith of those who believe, but they do nothing for those who don't. Jesus' listeners didn't want the salvation He offered if the terms were to admit their need for Him. They wanted miracles not as proof, but as a means of self-justification. They were really saying, "Why should we believe Him? After all, we don't have any proof that He's the Messiah." Of course they did. They could have proven He was the Messiah in an instant. How? By repenting and believing in Him as their Lord and Savior. They chose not to. They chose to put up a smoke screen in their minds, and Jesus read their minds.

They refused the only absolutely foolproof way the Jews in the synagogue (or anyone else) could have known Jesus was the Messiah, and it had nothing to do with miracles or healing people. They could, very simply, have admitted their sin, asked Him to save them, and seen whether or not they experienced the joyous blessing and clearing of conscience that comes to those who repent. They had no intention of doing that, and Jesus knew it.

## A BRILLIANT CONCESSION

In Luke 4:24, He said, "Assuredly, I say to you, no prophet is accepted in his own country." Instead of "Assuredly," some translations retain "Amen" from the Greek, meaning "I solemnly assure you." It's an idiom for "I'm telling you the truth. No prophet is welcome in his hometown; no prophet is *dektos*, accepted, in his hometown." Experts are always from out of town, aren't they? It's yet more proof that familiarity breeds contempt.

Jesus was making a bit of a concession. He was saying to them in so many words, "I can see it's hard for you to get past the fact that I'm a local guy, that I grew up here, that I am Joseph's son and Mary's boy, and that this is the synagogue you have seen Me in all the years of My life. I understand that." I think there's a bit of mercy in Jesus' words of understanding that no prophet is welcome in his home-town. He repeated that phrase a year and a half later, when He came back again to that synagogue, as recorded in Matthew 13:57 and Mark 6:4. It also appears in John 4:44.

Jesus made this concession in the light of human behavior being what it is. But then He made a brilliant and profound transition. He brought up two prophets, Elijah in Luke 4:25 and Elisha in verse 27, whom the people of Israel had hated, rejected, and refused. Jesus' hearers all knew of Elijah, the great prophet of Israel. During his ministry around 850 B.C., there were many widows. Moreover, Baal worship was going on everywhere because the king, Ahab, had mar-ried a pagan Baal worshipper named Jezebel. Ahab began worship-ping Baal under the influence of his wife, and soon the whole of Israel followed his example. Ahab was so bad, 1 Kings 16:33 says, that he "did more to provoke the LORD God of Israel to anger than all the kings of Israel who were before him."

Chapter 17 of 1 Kings begins with the prophet Elijah calling down the judgment of God upon Ahab and his subjects. Elijah prayed to the true God for a drought to prove that Baal, Ahab's god of rain and fertility, was a powerless god, false and impotent. God answered Elijah with a drought that lasted three-and-a-half years. In Luke 4:25–26, Jesus reminded His listeners of the fact that God sent Elijah to a des-titute widow in the town of Zarephath at the height of the drought, and he told her in the name of the Lord that if she shared the last of her food with him, the Lord would supply all her needs until the rains returned. She was obedient to the true God, despite having only enough flour and oil for one meager, final meal for herself and her son. She gave Elijah the food he requested.

This was a life-and-death decision for her. With no other support, she expected to starve after they had eaten the last morsels in the house. Sharing what little they had with this stranger would bring them to their desperate end even sooner. Yet, because she was obedient, God showed her His mercy, and from then until the drought was over, He miraculously replenished her flour bin and oil jar every day.

This story infuriated the Jews, because the widow of Zarephath was a Gentile in a culture that worshipped Baal, yet God bypassed many needy widows in Israel and sent Elijah only to this woman, who had made no effort at all to observe the religious laws with which the Israelites were so obsessed. It was her individual faith in the true God that mattered, not her tribal or religious pedigree. How is that possible? How could God bless a despicable Gentile in a pagan land, while seeming to ignore the law-abiding Jews? Outrageous!

Though the people in the synagogue were getting angrier by the moment, Jesus kept the truth coming. He went on in verse 27 to a story about Elisha, who succeeded Elijah, during a time from 850 to 790 B.C., when many lepers were in Israel. Leprosy was a sort of categorical word that covered a variety of ancient diseases that affected the skin described in Leviticus 13, everything from superficial problems to serious ones. It may also have included what we today call leprosy, that frightening malady also known as Hansen's disease.

These tended to be disfiguring diseases, and some could spread frighteningly fast. They made the victims unclean; they were cut off from all fellowship, social activity, and family contact, and they were isolated because others feared being stricken (though today with modern treatment, the risk of spreading Hansen's disease is considered negligible). Israel had many, many such rank outcasts, physically quarantined for their horrible maladies. It was in the time of Elisha, and they didn't like Elisha. He had no more honor in his own country than Elijah did. The people were still worshipping Baal, they were still turning their backs on the true and living God, and then along came leprosies everywhere. And Luke 4:27 says that God cleansed none of the lepers except Naaman the Syrian.

Oh, man, did the Jews hate this story! Naaman was a military commander in chief of a land known as Aram. He commanded terrorists who were always pillaging Israel. They crossed the border, carried out their raid, killed Jews, and took men and women prisoners back to Syria to use as slaves. Naaman was a violent enemy leader, like the modern Palestinian militants who attack the Jews. What's more, he was a Gentile, and he was a leper! He was about as despicable as people get.

On one of his raids, described in 2 Kings 5, he captured a girl and brought her back to be a slave to his wife. Amazingly, the girl had a compassionate attitude: she knew about his leprosy, and she told him he needed to go to Israel to find the man of God named Elisha, because God could heal through him. Naaman began to believe in the power of the God of Israel, and eventually, through a series of events, he wound up meeting Elisha.

Elisha said the God of Israel would heal Naaman if he immersed himself in the river seven times. The suggestion made Naaman furious. Here was a prideful figure who saw himself as a VIP, a man of great honor, a military leader of stature, dignity, and nobility. No way was he going to be demeaned by dunking himself seven times. He even complained at the thought of going in Elisha's dirty river, when he had a nice clean river back home.

But Naaman left Elisha's house and his servant said, "Well, better a dirty river and a clean Naaman, huh?" He started to have second thoughts. And he realized his desperation, realized that there was no relief and no cure, no healing except by the God of Israel. "Is this man of God really the man of God? Is God truly God? Is Elisha really His prophet?" Naaman was thinking, "How will I ever know unless I submit to what He asks? In my desperation, my destitution, and my disease, I have to do what the man tells me to do. Then I'll know whether he's the man of God and Israel's God is the True Deliverer."

So he went and did his seven dunks in Elisha's dirty river. Guess what? He was washed clean from every element of his leprosy!

If you were sitting in the synagogue at that moment, you were saying, "This is not going well. So, we are worse than a Gentile widow from Jezebel's hometown! We are worse than a Syrian Gentile terrorist leper! This is intolerable! God overlooks our widows and lepers and shows His grace to pagans. And He's going to pass us by now, if we don't embrace Jesus as Lord and Messiah."

## THE FRUIT OF SPIRITUAL PRIDE

It's not at all surprising that Luke 4:28 says the people in the synagogue, "when they heard these things, were filled with wrath." Nothing is worse than spiritual pride, because it is a barrier people selfishly put up that separates them from their own salvation. The Lord had said, "You know I come to save, and this is it. But I can save only the poor, the prisoners, the blind, and the oppressed. It doesn't matter whether one is a Gentile woman or a Syrian leper. It just matters that he sees his bankruptcy and destitution, and he comes to Me like the hated tax collector who pounded his guilt-ridden chest and cried: 'God, be merciful to me a sinner!' (Luke 18:13), or the man who said, 'Lord, I believe; help my unbelief!' (Mark 9:24). He may not know everything there is to know, and his faith may not be full, but if he will just come in his desperation and say, 'I don't have a choice. I see what I am, and I see what You can do for me,' then he will know I am the Messiah."

We can't know Jesus as the Messiah until we surrender to Him. I couldn't know Him as my Savior until I gave up my life to Him. Then I knew. Parading an infinite number of miracles in front of me wouldn't have proved anything. Miracles are beside the point. You will never know whether Jesus can save your soul from hell, give you new life, re-create your soul, plant His Holy Spirit there, forgive your sin, and send you to heaven until you give your life totally to Him. That is self-denial, cross bearing, and following Him in obedience.

All Jesus' listeners could think about was that in this story, they were less than the Gentiles. They were furious with Jesus, because He insisted that unless they saw themselves as no better than a terrorist Syrian leper, as no better than a pagan Gentile widow, as no better than outcasts, they weren't going to receive salvation. And that was absolutely intolerable to lifelong attenders of the synagogue— serious, devout Jews. It was unthinkable because they were so committed to the self-righteousness that came with believing they could work their way to salvation by their own merit and religion. How could they be humble when they were earning their way into heaven by being Jewish, loyal to traditional morality and religious law?

And so, as it says in Luke 4:29, they "rose up." All of a sudden bedlam broke loose in the crowded synagogue. They grabbed Jesus with the violence and blind hatred of a lynch mob and roared out of the city to the edge of a cliff. They were ready to throw Him over and watch Him splatter on the rocks below. Deuteronomy 13 told the Jews that they could kill a false prophet. They were so entrenched in their self-justifying pride, so unwilling to see their sin, that when Jesus came to them at last, they tried to kill Him. After waiting so long for their promised Messiah and King, they would rather destroy Him than have Him threaten their self-righteousness.

It always comes to this, though not so violently. There's only one reason why people who know the truth of the gospel are not willing to repent and believe. It is because they will not see themselves as the poor, prisoners, blind, and oppressed. It has nothing to do with the style of music your church offers, the drama and skits you stage, or the quality of your laser light show. It has everything to do with the spiritual deadness and blindness of pride. God offers nothing to people who are content with their own condition, except judgment. If you don't think you are headed for hell, don't think you need forgiveness, you put no value on the gospel of grace.

In their minds, these Jews in the synagogue were the respectable ones. They were the godly, the chosen, the true worshippers, the legally loyal, the ceremonialists, the covenantalists. Gentiles were wretched idolaters, destitute outcasts. The Jews could never see themselves as spiritual widows or lepers. Religious as they were, Jesus' relatives, friends, and neighbors hated what He said so much that they tried to kill Him! They hated that message so violently, because they refused to be humiliated. You can't preach salvation, lead anyone to salvation, or be saved yourself unless you're willing to be humiliated and recognize your sinful condition. Again, it's that matter of self-denial, isn't it?

They tried to murder Him, but it wasn't in their power, because it wasn't God's way or His time. Luke 4:30 describes a supernatural, instant calm: "Then passing through the midst of them, He went His way." We don't know how that happened. In some miraculous way, He just was gone. Here was the miracle they had demanded, but it took Him from their midst, symbolizing the judgment they brought on themselves by their hateful unbelief. How sad. What might have been for them—forgiveness and fullness of joy forever—they refused.

How about you? Do you want to know whether Jesus is who He claimed to be? First, you must come to grips with His diagnosis of *your* spiritual condition. Confess your utter sinfulness. Deny yourself, and give Him your life. That's the only way you'll ever know. Do you see yourself among the poor, prisoners, blind, and oppressed? If not, you can witness all the miracles under the sun, real or fake, you can see the whole parade of show-and-tell, and it's not going to convince you. There's only one way to know that Jesus can save your soul from hell, change your life, and send you to eternal heaven with all your sins forgiven. That one way is to be honest and desperate enough to admit your sin. That's the only kind of person Jesus can save. Take your meager, wicked life and hand it over to Him, and see what He does with it. That's what you have to do, and that's the invitation you have to proclaim.

## TRUE FREEDOM

Probably nothing is more true of sinners today than that they think they are free. They see Christianity as some kind of bondage. It is all about rights: "No one is going to infringe on my rights. I can be what I want to be. I'm free to be myself." You hear that inane statement again and again.

Such people are not free. The Bible defines them as prisoners. Sin has indebted them to God, and it's a debt they cannot pay. They are in bondage, and they are awaiting eternal death. According to Hebrews 2:15, Satan wields the power of death and holds captive "those who through fear of death [are] all their lifetime subject to bondage." They are the children of wrath; Ephesians 2:2 calls them "sons of disobedience" who are under the power of, and in bondage to, their own sin. The divine sentence on them is incarceration for eternity in hell, where they will never die.

The real Sovereign over them, the real Judge who has imprisoned them, called them guilty, and sentenced them to death, is God Himself. It is God who destroys both soul and body in hell. The sinner is a prisoner of Satan and sin, but more than that, he's a prisoner of God, the eternal Executioner, who is holding him accountable and has him awaiting a horrific, unending death.

That's the choice: eternal death or eternal life. To gain eternal life, you have to let go of your spiritual pride, and die to yourself. To lead others to Christ, to save them from this eternal judgment, you have to speak that truth in love; you have to tell them the truth without pulling any punches. Does that seem impossible? Will your audience turn you off? Well, as we can see, they turned Jesus off. In fact, they hated His message so much, His own neighbors and relatives, in a rage, tried to kill him for preaching it.

If you suffer for the truth of the gospel, and you will, remember you're in good company. You're following the best example who ever served God; you are on the Lord's side, casting off self-righteousness to walk through the narrow gospel gate that leads to eternal life, and faithfully giving that gospel to others.

## A VALUE BEYOND PRICE

Some of us are fortunate enough, by God's grace, to experience a few moments on this earth when the preciousness of the gospel manifests itself with life-changing clarity. In those moments we realize that preserving and sharing the message of salvation is worth any cost, because its value is beyond any price.

When I was in college, I spoke at a banquet where I received a football award. I gave my testimony of my love for Christ. Somebody came up to me afterward and said, "I know of a girl in the hospital you could help. She needs to hear what you have to say."

I was not a pastor, and I hadn't had any sort of serious counselor training. I was a twenty-one-year-old college football player. But I told this man I would make a visit. So I went to the hospital, and there I met a cute seventeen-year-old cheerleader named Polly. Her boyfriend had accidentally shot her through the neck and severed her spinal cord. She was paralyzed for life.

She was lying, covered up, on a sheepskin to minimize bedsores. I introduced myself and explained that someone asked me to come. Then I said, "I can't imagine what you're going through."

The first words out of her mouth were: "I'd kill myself if I could. I have no reason to live."

Not knowing what else to do, I started into a presentation of the gospel. "It's not what happens to your body that matters, Polly, it's what happens to your eternal soul. You're going to live forever somewhere. God can bring joy into your heart even now if the issue of your soul is taken care of. Would you like to hear about how that can happen?"

She said, "Sure. Okay. I'm desperate."

So I unfolded the gospel, what Christ had done on the cross and that He asked for her life. Talk about a serious conversation! When I finished, I said, "Polly, would you be interested in confessing Jesus Christ as your Lord and following Him, and receiving His forgiveness and eternal life?"

She said, "I would. I don't know where else to turn."

So we prayed together, and I went back to see her again several times. On one of those visits she told me, "You know, John, in some ways I'm glad this accident happened. If it hadn't, I would never have met Jesus Christ."

As terribly as she had suffered, Polly was beginning to sense that what she could gain in the way of eternal life was more than worth the price of physical suffering in this life. And I said to myself, "*This matters*. Running around on a field with a piece of pig under my arm to the screams of the crowd doesn't matter. *This matters*."

Because of that episode and one other I'll share a little later, life took on a completely different tone for me. The fact that God had allowed Polly to respond to that gospel presentation gave me the realization that He could use me in that way. She became a follower of Jesus Christ and eventually met and married a wonderful Christian man. As I look back at my life, my experience with her had a major impact on my decision to serve the Lord of the gospel. After that exposure to the power of the gospel, I thought, *This is all I want for my life. Nothing else even comes close in significance.*

# 5

## HIGHWAY TO HEAVEN

It was the famous baseball player Yogi Berra who offered the following advice with all seriousness, "If you come to a fork in the road, take it!" That's not helpful, because the choice of direction has consequences. All of life concentrates on mankind at the crossroads. And since we're always at a decision point about something, it's fair to say we're always at a crossroads. Most of the choices are inconsequential: Red shirt or blue shirt? Return this phone call first or that one? Regular or super-size? Original or extra crispy? Some are much more important: Where should you go to school? Whom will you marry? Where will you live? What career path will you follow?

Inevitably we face a final choice that determines the ultimate consequence—how we will spend eternity: whether we will follow the world through the wide, inviting gate that leads to destruction and eternal punishment, or follow Jesus through the narrow gate that leads to eternal joy in heaven.

God confronts sinners with this ultimate choice. They are *responsible* for choosing, yet so hopelessly mired in sin that no one ever chooses rightly without divine enablement. Even so, God pleads with sinners to choose Christ over unbelief; reconciliation with God, not enmity with Him; repentance rather than sin; and life instead of death. Through Moses, God confronted the children of Israel in Deuteronomy 30:15–16: "See, I have set before you today life and good, death and evil, in that I command you today to love the LORD your God, to walk in His ways, and to keep His commandments, His statutes, and His judgments, that you may live and multiply." God gave Israel the ultimate choice—life or death, good or evil—and called for a decision.

Joshua, who followed Moses in leading the Israelites as they entered the promised land, said in Joshua 24:15, "And if it seems evil to you to serve the LORD, choose for yourselves this day whom you will serve, whether the gods which your fathers served that were on the other side of the River, or the gods of the Amorites, in whose land you dwell. But as for me and my house, we will serve the LORD." God asked, "Will it be the false gods, or will it be Me?"

In Jeremiah 21:8, the prophet heard God say, "Behold, I set before you the way of life and the way of death." Elijah on Mount Carmel called for a decision in 1 Kings 18:21: "And Elijah came to all the people, and said, 'How long will you falter between two opinions? If the LORD is God, follow Him; but if Baal, follow him.'"

We make this choice at the crossroads of Christ: choose life or choose death. That's what Jesus said in Matthew 7:13–14, in His famous and often-misunderstood Sermon on the Mount: "Enter by the narrow gate; for wide is the gate and broad is the way that leads to destruction, and there are many who go in by it. Because narrow is the gate and difficult is the way which leads to life, and there are few who find it."

We looked briefly at this provocative and vivid invitation earlier on, but it's an essential truth worth digging deeper into. This eternity-defining crossroads, this choice of one way or the other, is the climax Jesus was driving toward throughout this great sermon of indictment against the self-righteous legalism and works salvation system of the

Pharisees; a calling of His people to true faith and salvation. The imagery in the Lord's analogy is simple. There are two gates, leading to two roads, ending in two destinations, populated by two different crowds. Here the Lord focused on the inevitable decision you, I, and the rest of the world have before us.

## THE NO-CHOICE CHOICE

Too many contemporary Christian churches have completely abandoned the idea of the necessity of choice, insisting there's room for a diversity of opinion on the faith. As the war with Iraq got under way in 2003, a mainline Protestant church in New York, displaying its happy ambivalence, supported some members who volunteered for a promilitary Adopt-a-Soldier campaign, and at the same time it encouraged others who participated in antimilitary protest rallies. The rector explained, "We're trying to cover all the bases. I don't want the war in Iraq to cause a war in my congregation."

Numerous churches take the same approach to the gospel, refusing to say anything definitive about the way of salvation and never confronting those who are following the broad road. As Randall Balmer, professor of American religious history at Barnard College in New York, observed, "It's a market economy." To keep attendance and membership from slipping, church leaders are poaching each other's "customers" the way the local bank or supermarket would, by catering to their personal preferences, by "covering all the bases." How can people ever find the narrow gate to heaven, if so many of their own churches choose not to make the choice between Christ's way and the world's way clear?

The church can't stand behind multiple points of view and be legitimate. If the Christian gospel is true, everything else is a lie. If Christ alone saves, those who do not believe in Him are doomed. The church can't lead sinners to salvation if it presents one road as being as good as another. Yet I hear this inclusivism all the time from so-called Christians. If you're afraid of causing discord by upholding the narrow exclusivity of Jesus' message, that is the same as choosing the broad way. The gospel is exclusive. Jesus is the only way. The gate is that narrow.

## ONLY TWO RELIGIONS

There are two things you cannot do with this sermon Jesus preached on the mount. One is, you can't stand back and admire it, though many do. Jesus is not interested in having people admire His ethics; He wants us to follow Him on the narrow road. The second thing is that you can't push this decision into some nebulous tomorrow. Jesus calls sinners to repentance now.

As the King of kings, Christ came to bring the world a unique and special kingdom separate from all others. He knew we couldn't understand His kingdom unless He explained its principles, and that's why He gave this masterful sermon. At this climactic moment, He was saying, "Here's what My kingdom is all about. Here is what authentic faith looks like. Are you in or out?" He demands a response. And the choice is utterly clear-cut: the narrow gate, or the wide gate. No other alternatives exist.

John Stott wrote in *Basic Christianity*, "Whatever his parentage and upbringing, every responsible adult is obliged to make up his own mind for or against Christ. We cannot remain neutral. Nor can we drift into Christianity. Nor can anybody else settle the matter for us. We must decide for ourselves."[1] We naturally look for accommodation and compromise, because we want everybody to agree. We love the gray area. It seems nicer. But Jesus says there is no gray area; it's one or the other.

When I'm interviewed by a TV network, or in any fast-paced situation where I've got to make my point in a fifteen-second sound bite, I want to say two black-and-white things: I want to proclaim the absolute and single authority of Scripture, and the absolute exclusivity of Jesus Christ. It's kind of a response to the electronic version of Broadway producer David Belasco's challenge: "If you can't write your idea on the back of my business card, you don't have an idea." Like it or not, I've got only a few seconds to make my point, and that forces me to think about what are the most important, most fundamental tenets of the faith.

There I am, with monitors flashing and technicians moving around just off camera; the host is listening to me with one ear, and to his producer through an earpiece in the other; we're jammed together on this tiny set with our knees bumping; and when the host levels his laser-beam gaze at me and says, "Before we go to a commercial, what do you think about that, John?" I'd better know what I think. I think the world needs to know the Bible is the only truth of God, and Jesus Christ the only Savior.

Of course, other guests typically have different agendas. When I was on the air with Deepak Chopra, he wanted to engage me in a battle over New Testament manuscripts. Another time, a Catholic priest tried to debate the meaning of a parable. I let them have their turn—politely, I hope—and then changed the subject back where it needed to be: authority of Scripture and exclusivity of Christ.

Every argument eventually works its way around to those two unflinching, unbreachable truths of the genuine gospel. They reveal that there is only one true religion and the rest is false, and that there is the right and all else is wrong. All the way through the Sermon on the Mount, Jesus contrasted the true religion of Christ with the false Judaism of the scribes and Pharisees and their followers. He offered not a lot of choices, only two. The gospel saves; anything and everything else condemns.

## DIVINE VERSUS HUMAN RIGHTEOUSNESS

There's a common misconception that the choice between Christ and false gods is the choice between desiring to go to hell and desiring to go to heaven. I've heard preachers say the narrow way is the way of Christianity that people choose when they want to go to heaven, and the broad way is the way people choose who are content to go to hell. But they are misinformed or confused. It is not a contrast between godliness and Christianity on one hand and irreligious, lewd, lascivious pagan masses headed merrily for hell on the other. It is a contrast between two kinds of religions, both roads marked "This Way to Heaven." Satan doesn't put up a sign that says, "Hell—Exit Here." That's not his style. People on the broad road think that road goes to heaven.

It's also a contrast between divine righteousness and human righteousness, between divine religion and human religion, thus between true religion and false religion. God's Word described the Pharisees' problem in Luke 18:9, which says that they "trusted in themselves that they were righteous." It was a religion of human righteousness. They worshipped themselves. And that was inadequate, because they weren't righteous enough to meet the high standard of God's kingdom. Only Jesus can do that.

The choice we all make is this: either we're good enough on our own, through our belief system and morality, to make it to heaven; or we're not, and we have to cast ourselves on the mercy of God through Christ to get there. Those are the only two systems of religion in the world. One is a religion of human merit; the other recognizes that we find true merit in Christ alone, and it comes to the sinner only by grace. There may be a thousand different religious names and terms, but only two religions really exist. There is the truth of divine accomplishment, which says God has done it all in Christ, and there is the lie of human achievement, which says we have some sort of hand in saving ourselves. One is the religion of grace, the other the religion of works. One offers salvation by faith alone; the other offers salvation by the flesh.

Man-made and demon-designed systems of religion are based on the assumption that we don't really need a Savior, or aren't fully dependent on Him, because we have the capacity to develop our own righteousness. Just let God give us a little religious environment to aid our natural goodness, dispense a little power to us, or infuse a little strength into us. Give us a few rules, a few religious routines and rituals, and we'll crank up salvation on our own. The lie of human achievement comes under myriad different titles, but it's all the same system, because it's spawned out of the same source: Satan himself. He packages it in different boxes, but it's all the same product. On the other hand, the truth of divine accomplishment is Christianity. And it stands alone.

Tragically, most of humanity is religiously speeding down the wide highway of human achievement, convinced it's headed toward some fabulous heavenly destiny because of its own basic goodness, noble works, and religious deeds. By contrast, Jesus said the only true way to heaven is the narrow pathway of trusting Him alone as Lord and Savior.

The Jews taught that they could make it on their own. That's why it was so shocking when the apostle Paul said, "Therefore by the deeds of the law no flesh will be justified in His sight" (Rom. 3:20). He also said that the law came in order to stop our mouths from any claim to righteousness and to render the whole world guilty before God. The Law came to show us our sinfulness, but when self-righteous, ego-centered man saw that he was sinful by the Law, he didn't want to face his sinfulness. Fallen people set the Law of God aside, constantly inventing new systems that accommodate their short-comings, then affirming that they are okay before their gods, based on their own personal criteria or religious beliefs and behaviors.

The Lord's whole thrust in the Sermon on the Mount, particularly with this key point of the wide and narrow gates, is to break the backs of such deadly kinds of belief systems and show that everyone who believes those lies is wrong. Jesus' purpose was to bring His listeners or readers to where He began the sermon: the truly blessed are the poor in spirit; blessed are they who mourn, blessed are the meek, blessed are those who hunger and thirst after righteousness. He started out where He wanted to end up, with people who are broken, mourning over their total sinfulness, meek in the face of God and the Law, hungering and thirsting for what they know they don't have but desperately need: the righteousness of God.

But the Pharisees were never tuned to that message. In Luke 18:11 one of them prayed, "God, I thank You that I am not like other men" and bragged about how he fasted and tithed. Yet he never expressed any sin or remorse to God, because he thought he was so good, he had nothing to feel guilty about and no condemnation from which to be saved. And in the corner, on the other hand, was that man we've mentioned before, pounding on his chest and saying, "God, be merciful to me a sinner." Jesus said, "This man went down to his house justified rather than the other" (Luke 18:14). Jesus wants to bring us to a point where we realize our utter incapacity to please God in our own flesh and cry out in desperation with a broken spirit, meek and mourning, for righteousness from God. The Jews thought they were righteous and on their way to heaven and the kingdom. Just the opposite was true. What a delusion! Jesus forced them to rethink their choice.

## NARROW-MINDED ACTION

In Matthew 7:13–14, Jesus mentioned the narrow gate twice and the wide gate once. From the intersection, both roads look as if they lead to salvation. Both promise the pathway to God, to the kingdom, glory, blessing, heaven. But only one of the roads really goes there. The other is paved with self-righteousness as a substitute for the perfect righteousness God demands in Matthew 5:48: "Therefore you shall be perfect, just as your Father in heaven is perfect." Either you accept the truth that salvation comes from what God has done for you in Christ, or you will be left with nothing but your own sinful self-righteousness.

The main characteristic of the way of life Jesus pointed to was its narrowness. The broad way had all kinds of tolerance for sin, for laws beyond the law of God, and standards below and beyond the standards of God. Every man-made religious system is part of the scenery of the broad way. But Jesus didn't look for ways to compromise. He simply said, "You've got to get off that broad road. You must enter this narrow way. If you're going to be in the kingdom, you've got to come on these terms."

It is not enough to listen to preaching about the gate; it is not enough to respect the ethics; you've got to walk through the gate. And you can't come unless you abandon your self-righteousness, see yourself as a beggar in spirit, mourning over sin, meek before a holy God, not proud and boastful, hungering and thirsting for righteousness, and not believing you have it. Hell will be full of people who thought highly of the Sermon on the Mount. You must do more than that. You must obey it and take action.

You can't stand outside and admire the narrow gate; you've got to drop everything and walk through it. There's that self-denial again. You come through, stripped of everything. But isn't that narrow-minded? Does that mean Christianity doesn't allow room for opposing viewpoints? No compassionate tolerance? No diversity?

That's exactly right. We don't do it that way because we're selfish or prideful or egotistical; we do it that way because that's what God said to do. If God said there were forty-eight ways to salvation, I'd preach and write about all forty-eight of them. But there aren't:

"Nor is there salvation in any other, for there is no other name under heaven given among men by which we must be saved," Acts 4:12 reminds us, no other name but Jesus.

In John's gospel, Jesus said, "I am the bread of life" (6:35); "I am the way, the truth, and the life" (14:6); "He who does not enter the sheepfold by the door . . . is a thief and a robber . . . I am the door" (10:1, 7). Paul affirmed these words in 1 Timothy 2:5: "For there is one God and one Mediator between God and men, the Man Christ Jesus." There's only one: Christ and Christ alone. That's a narrow viewpoint. But that is Christianity. And it is the truth. You have to enter on God's terms, through God's prescribed gate. Christ is that gate. Holy God has the right to determine the basis of salvation, and He has determined that it is Jesus Christ and Him alone. You can enter only through Him, by faith.

## ONE AT A TIME

He has also decided that His people are to pass through the narrow gate alone. This is implicit in the text, which some commentators say is best expressed by the idea of a turnstile. If you've ever been to the zoo or a ball game with a group of people, you probably had to go through a turnstile. And when you crowd up at the gate, everybody's in a big hurry, trying to get in at once, but you soon realize that going through a turnstile is not a group activity. You've got to go one at a time. That's the way it is with a narrow gate. Walking through the gate to the kingdom of Christ is a solitary journey.

The Jews believed otherwise. They thought, "Hey, we're in the kingdom! We made it not as worthy individual followers of the Messiah, but as members of a worthy group based on Abrahamic heritage, Jewish ancestry, and circumcision." Like the Jews Jesus was preaching to, many people today believe that when they went to church, they automatically got on the tour bus to heaven; they'll just go in with the group. But there are no groups in a turnstile. You go through all alone. Salvation is individual.

That idea is hard to swallow, because we spend our lives rushing around with the crowd, being a part of the gang, part of the system, gaining acceptance. Then, all of a sudden, Christ tells you you're going to have to walk through this turnstile all by yourself. To a Pharisee that meant having to say good-bye to that cherished system and stepping out alone. Suddenly he's noticed that it isn't enough to claim his Abrahamic ancestry, it isn't enough to refer back to his circumcision. And it isn't enough to say, "I was born in a Christian family, I've been in the church all my life." As Laurence J. Peter mused, being in church doesn't make you a Christian any more than being in the garage makes you a car. You must come to Jesus alone, in an individual commitment to penitent, self-denying faith. That's hard.

## A BOGUS INVITATION

I know this shocks some people, because we hear all the time that getting saved is easy. "Just sign this little card!" "Just raise your hand!" "Just walk down that aisle while the choir sings one more stanza!" "Just recite this prayer." "Just ask Jesus into your heart." It all sounds simple. The only problem is that none of those actions has anything to do with real salvation and getting through the narrow gate. That sort of invitationalism implies that Jesus is some poor pitiful Savior, waiting for us to make the first move to allow Him His way. It implies that salvation hinges on a human decision, as if the power that saves us were the power of human "free will."

This emphasis is a peculiarly American phenomenon that started in the nineteenth century with a New York lawyer-turned-evangelist named Charles Finney. He was the most formidable American anti-Calvinist, and he insisted that people get saved by an act of sheer willpower. Therefore, whatever is necessary in order to manipulate their wills is an essential method, because whatever it takes to convince them to decide to be saved is legitimate. The end justifies the means. And so the manipulative "altar call" became a major focus of his evangelism.

Up to that time, American evangelists were, for the most part, Calvinistic, that is, they believed that sinners are saved by hearing the message of the gospel while God the Holy Spirit awakens them from sinful deadness. But Finney took a different path. He made emotional appeals and taught that salvation required no sovereign regeneration by God, but only the act of the human will. The people came streaming down the aisle under the force of his cleverness. The vast majority of these weren't real conversions; in fact, Finney later admitted that his ministry had produced mostly halfhearted and temporary "converts." But the spectacle of crowds surging forward was very convincing.

Dwight L. Moody picked up the technique from Finney, and he passed it along to a generation of stadium evangelists and ministry leaders who still stage sometimes enormous public events and manipulate people to come to the stage. Most of that activity is fruitless. No doubt I believe that, in spite of the manipulation and not because of it, some of the people who take a pledge, sign a card, or come down front at those services are brokenhearted, aware of their sinfulness, and ready to follow Jesus as Lord by bearing their crosses with total self-denial. Those are the people who will be taken in at the narrow gate by the power of God through the truth, who will find themselves on the highway to heaven. The rest will not, but may be deceived.

According to Jesus, it's very, very difficult to be saved. At the end of Matthew 7:14, He said of the narrow gate, "There are few who find it." I don't believe anyone ever slipped and fell into the kingdom of God. That's cheap grace, easy-believism, Christianity Lite, a shallow, emotional revivalist approach: "I believe in Jesus!" "Fine, you're part of the family, come on in!" No. The few who find the narrow gate have to search hard for it, then come through it alone. It's hard to find a church or preacher—or a Christian—who can direct you to it. The kingdom is for those who agonize to enter it, whose hearts are shattered over their sinfulness, who mourn in meekness, who hunger and thirst and long for God to change their lives. It's hard because you've got all hell against you. One of Satan's pervasive lies in the world today is that it's easy to become a Christian. It's not easy at all. It's a very narrow gate that you must find and go through alone, anguished over your sinfulness and longing for forgiveness.

Somebody might say this sounds like the religion of human achievement. Not so. When you come to brokenness, the recognition that you, of yourself, cannot make it through the narrow gate, then Christ pours into you grace upon grace to strengthen you for that entrance. In your brokenness, His power becomes your resource. Our part is to admit our sin and inability and plead for mercy and power from on high.

## NO BAGGAGE

You can't go through a turnstile with baggage. To get through the narrow gate that leads to heaven, you leave all your possessions behind and enter empty-handed. It's not the gate of the self-contented, who want to carry all their stuff in with them; it's the gate of the self-denying, who strip off all self-righteousness and self-reliance. Rejecting all they have been, they leave their former lives behind. Otherwise, they can't get through the gate. Nor can anybody else.

The rich young ruler made it to the gate and asked Jesus what he had to do to enter the kingdom. The Lord told him to drop his matched set of Gucci luggage and come on through. He had found the gate that few people ever find, but he refused to enter because he was too selfish and self-centered to make the sacrifice Jesus asked of him.

The point here is wonderfully expressed in Matthew 18:3, where Jesus says, "Unless you are converted and become as little children, you will by no means enter the kingdom of heaven." The distinctive mark of children is that they are utterly dependent on others and have achieved nothing of merit themselves. As the hymn writer puts it, "Nothing in my hand I bring, simply to Thy cross I cling." Saving faith is more than an act of the mind; it is a disdain for one's sinful self, an admission of unworthiness, a naked plea: "Lord, be merciful to me, a sinner!" There's nothing wrong with raising our hands or saying a little prayer, but those things do not bring true salvation apart from authentic faith in Christ. Jesus called for a narrow, difficult, radical, dramatic admission of sinfulness; an acknowledgment that we are nothing and have nothing with which to commend ourselves to God. Faith begins when we throw ourselves on His mercy for forgiveness.

## REPENTANCE AND SURRENDER

To come through the narrow gate, you must enter with your heart repentant over sin, ready to turn from loving sin to loving the Lord. When John the Baptist was preparing a people to receive the Messiah, they were coming to be baptized because they wanted to have their sins forgiven. To any Jew, preparation for the coming of the Messiah and readiness for His kingdom meant purging the heart of its sinfulness.

You must also enter the narrow gate in utter surrender to Christ. No one can be regenerate, as Christ indicates in Matthew 7, by simply adding Jesus Christ to his carnal activities. Salvation is not an addition; it's a transformation that leads to willing submission to His Word. The whole message of 1 John is that if you are truly redeemed, it will manifest itself in a transformed life in which you confess sin, characteristically obey the Lord, and manifest love for the Lord and others. The divine miracle of a changed life reveals true salvation, resulting in a heart that desires to obey the Lord. As Jesus said, "If you abide in My word, you are My disciples indeed" (John 8:31).

If someone who calls himself a Christian doesn't think and act like a Christian, he's not on the road he thinks he is. He has likely joined the mighty band rushing through the wide gate of false religion. He exhibits none of this self-denial stuff: "Hey, bring all your baggage, your personal ambition, your will, your selfish desires, your immorality, your lack of repentance, your reluctance even to submit fully to the leadership of Christ! You can just come right on through the gate of self-indulgence!" Many claim to be Christians and yet are totally self-indulgent. They will never get through the narrow gate with all that baggage. Though they may not know it, they are on the broad road to destruction.

## STANDING AT THE CROSSROADS

Once you've come in the wide gate, the whole gang's there and life is easy: no rules, no rigid morality, and plenty of tolerance and diversity just as long as you say you love Jesus. All the desires of the fallen heart are fed on that road. There's no need for humility, or to study the Word of God. It takes absolutely no effort; as with a dead fish floating downstream, the current does it all. It's what Ephesians 2:2 describes as "the course of this world." It's the broad road where "the way of the ungodly shall perish" (Ps. 1:6).

Contrast this with the narrow way. The best translation of the text in Matthew 7:13–14 would be a "constricted" way. It literally means to press together or be confined, as in a narrow place on a precipice. That's why Paul said in Ephesians that we must walk circumspectly, with our eyes open, and not wander around. It's a very restricted way, hemmed in on both sides by the chastening hand of God. You step off this side and—*whack*—you get your spiritual knuckles hit! Same on the other side. The requirements are firm, strict, refined, and clear-cut, and there's no room for any deviation or departure from them. It must be the desire of our hearts to fulfill them, knowing full well that when we fail, God will chasten, and then God will wonderfully and lovingly forgive and set us on our feet again to pursue His will.

The choice, then, is between these two destinations: the broad way that leads to destruction, and the narrow way that is the only highway to heaven. All forms of the religion of human achievement—from humanism and atheism (the ultimate religion of human achievement, where man himself is God) to pseudo-Christianity—are going to end up in the same hell. As John Bunyan said, "For some the entrance to hell is from the portals of heaven." What a shock it's going to be for some people. On the other hand, the narrow way is going to open up into eternal bliss. The broad way narrows down into a terrible pit. The narrow way widens into the endless glories of heaven, the fullness of an unspeakable, everlasting, unclouded fellowship of joy with God that we can't even imagine.

In Matthew 10:32–33, Jesus said, "Therefore whoever confesses Me before men, him I will also confess before My Father who is in heaven. But whoever denies Me before men, him I will also deny before My Father who is in heaven." Are you willing to confess the Christ of the New Testament, who is the true Christ, and the gospel He proclaimed, which is the true gospel? Are you unashamed, so that you will openly and publicly confess them? Or are you ashamed of Him and His words, and consequently you deny that He is who He says He is or that His gospel is the true message? If you are a denier, if you are ashamed of Him; if the preaching of the cross is, to you, foolish, then you are among the perishing.

Admiration is not enough. Saying you appreciate Christ and you serve Christ are not enough. Many on the broad road are those who have admired Jesus, but they didn't come through the narrow gate. They didn't come with broken and contrite hearts. They didn't come crushed under the weight of the law of God with a penitent attitude, embracing their true condition as desperate and damned, and crying out for salvation from the only source: the Lord Jesus Christ.

The Lord says, "If you don't know Me on My terms, I don't know you at all. If you haven't come in repentance, conviction of your own sin, and abandonment of self with such desperation that you cry out for salvation and righteousness and heaven, whatever the cost, then you didn't pass through the narrow gate. You haven't come humbly seeking forgiveness, knowing you don't deserve it." You were virtually ashamed of Jesus and His words, and you'll find Him ashamed of you.

## THE ETERNAL CHOICE

Jesus told us very specifically that this shame will be manifest "when He comes" (Luke 9:26). When a sinner dies today, he ends up in hell immediately. He doesn't have to wait for the return of Jesus Christ for that. It is almost like being in prison before his final sentence. When somebody commits a crime, he is caught and waits in prison for the final adjudication and sentencing.

That final sentencing will come when Christ returns in His glory. He will come for His church, but His glory will not be manifest in the earth. The church will disappear in the Rapture, followed by a terrible time of Great Tribulation, and then Jesus will come back in shining glory. At the Second Coming, He will return to earth to set up His rule in full display of the glory of the Father, "revealed from heaven with His mighty angels, in flaming fire" (2 Thess. 1:7–8).

Jesus comes in His glory, the angels come in their glory, and perhaps the flaming fire also speaks of the Father, who was manifest many times in the Old Testament in the flame of fire that led Israel by night. The fire that Moses and the children of Israel saw on Sinai also represented God: the shining, magnificent, blazing fire of His presence.

Matthew described this, too, referring numerous times to Jesus "coming in glory." When He comes, He will be dealing out retribution to those who do not know God. If you don't obey the gospel, you can't know God. There isn't any other way to be saved.

He's going to deal out the punishment on all nonbelievers as described in 2 Thessalonians 1:9: "These shall be punished with everlasting destruction from the presence of the Lord and from the glory of His power." This means they will undergo a nonterminal, everlasting destruction away from God's presence and experience eternal weeping and wailing and gnashing of teeth. When Jesus comes in His glory to earth at the Second Coming, the end of human history as we know it, the destruction of the ungodly will take place.

Then the Lord will set up His millennial kingdom, and at the end of the thousand years of the kingdom, the actual final tribunal will come. Revelation 20 gives us the story. John, looking into that future at the end of the kingdom, envisioned the final event in the universe as we know it. He saw a "great white throne and Him who sat on it, from whose face the earth and the heaven fled away" (v. 11). Peter wrote of it as the elements of the universe melting with fervent heat (2 Pet. 3:10). That is the uncreation of the universe. It just disappears. God will uncreate the entire universe out of existence faster than He created it.

John saw the dead, great and small, significant and insignificant, brought before the throne. The books were opened, which identifies the fact that God has a perfect assessment of everything in all our lives. And there was another book open, the Book of Life, in which those who are saved have their names written. God will judge the dead from the things written in the books according to their deeds. That's tragic, because their deeds are evil.

John recorded that the sea gave up the dead in it, Death and Hades gave up the dead in them. The dead literally will come, with resurrected bodies prepared for eternal pain, before this great throne, and God will judge every one of them by his deeds, because that's all He can use to judge them. Judged by our deeds, we are all doomed. Revelation 20:14: "Then Death and Hades were cast into the lake of fire." This lake of fire is the second death, and anyone whose name was not written in the Book of Life was thrown in the flaming lake for an eternity of agony.

The only way to escape the lake of fire is to have your name in the Book of Life. Your name being there doesn't mean you didn't commit any deeds of sin; it means the sacrifice of Christ covered and paid for those actions.

When Christ comes in His glory, when He comes in the glory of the Father and the holy angels, when He comes to deal with the ungodly, to destroy them, to punish them with eternal punishment, to bring them before the final tribunal for their final sentencing, it is at that point that the Lord will manifest that He is finally and forever ashamed of all those who were ashamed of Him and His gospel.

It is a frighteningly serious reality. And understanding what is at stake, why would anyone ever stake eternity on pop Christianity, which won't get you to and through the narrow gate? What benefit, what profit is there if you gain the whole world, fulfilling all the lust of the flesh, the lust of the eyes, and the pride of life—if you were to get them all—if it means losing your eternal soul and burning for eternity in a lake of fire? Far better to come through the narrow gate.

Help us, Lord, to be awakened by Your Holy Spirit, that we may see ourselves as nothing but the worst of sinners, destitute beggars willing even to die, knowing that if we see ourselves thus and embrace Christ, we will be princes with God forever.

# 6

## Empty Words

Don't believe anyone who says it's easy to become a Christian. Salvation for sinners cost God His own Son; it cost God's Son His life, and it'll cost you the same thing. Salvation isn't gained by reciting mere words. Saving faith transforms the heart, and that in turn transforms behavior. Faith's fruit is seen in actions, not intentions. There's no room for passive spectators: words without actions are empty and futile. Remember that what John saw in his vision of judgment was a Book of Life, not a Book of Words or Book of Intellectual Musings. The life we live, not the words we speak, reveals whether our faith is authentic.

To come to God on God's terms requires us to recognize our own total unworthiness and inability, and that means the death of pride and self. That's hard because this fallen world, with its selfish bias, constantly tells us that we ought to love ourselves. We say, "Oh no, we love God more!" but our actions prove otherwise.

C. S. Lewis, who called pride "the great sin," and "spiritual cancer," wrote:

It is Pride which has been the chief cause of misery in every nation and every family since the world began . . . Pride always means enmity—it *is* enmity. And not only enmity between man and man, but enmity to God.

In God you come up against something which is in every respect immeasurably superior to yourself. Unless you know God as that—and therefore know yourself as nothing in comparison— you do not know God at all. As long as you are proud you cannot know God. A proud man is always looking down on things and people: and, of course, as long as you are looking down, you cannot see something that is above you.

That raises a terrible question. How is it that people who are quite obviously eaten up with Pride can say they believe in God and appear to themselves very religious? I am afraid it means they are worshipping an imaginary God.[1]

At the end of the Sermon on the Mount, after stating all the principles and warning about the false prophets, the Lord said effectively, "Now let Me warn you about one other thing: make sure you're not kidding yourself. Are you really a true member of the kingdom of heaven?" In Matthew 7:21–23, the Lord described the self-deception that comes from a mere verbal profession of faith: "Not everyone who says to Me, 'Lord, Lord,' shall enter the kingdom of heaven, but he who does the will of My Father in heaven. Many will say to Me in that day, 'Lord, Lord, have we not prophesied in Your name, cast out demons in Your name, and done many wonders in Your name?' And then I will declare to them, 'I never knew you; depart from Me, you who practice lawlessness!'"

Jesus made strong demands of those who desired to enter the kingdom, principles that we can sum up in one word: *righteousness*. Matthew 5:20 makes it clear: "For I say to you, that unless your righteousness exceeds the righteousness of the scribes and Pharisees, you will by no means enter the kingdom of heaven."

Matthew 7:21–22 denotes a verbal profession: "Not everyone

who says . . . Many will say to Me . . ." These are the people who say they're Christians, but they aren't; they *say* but don't *do*. The verses that follow, which we'll consider in the next chapter, highlight those who have only an intellectual knowledge: "Whoever hears these sayings . . . everyone who hears these sayings of Mine . . ." They *hear* but don't do. In one sense it's a verbal profession, and in another sense it's an intellectual knowledge, but neither produces the good fruit of a righteous life. They're nothing but empty words and empty hearts.

## THE GREAT DELUSION

Matthew 7:21 says that only "he who does the will of My Father in heaven" will enter the kingdom. If you do not live a genuinely righteous life, it doesn't matter what you claim. You are deceived. Both of the closing paragraphs to this great sermon, verses 21–23 and 24–27, contrast a right and a wrong response to the invitation of Christ, and they show that the choice we make determines our eternal destiny.

Remember that the Lord wasn't speaking to irreligious people here, but to people who were obsessed with religious activity. They were not apostates, heretics, atheists, or agnostics; they were extremely religious people. But they were damned because they were self-deluded and on the wrong road. Their self-delusion could have risen from their sitting under the teaching of a false prophet, or they could have learned the truth yet deluded themselves anyway.

This is an important issue, because I am convinced that the visible church today is literally jammed full of people who aren't Christians but don't know it. When I hear statistics such as two billion people in the world are Christians and two billion aren't, then I wonder who has established the criteria for being Christian. The

Bible says many take the broad road, but few take the narrow way to Christ. Most opinion polls report that almost half of the American people claim to be born-again Christians, but that doesn't square with the Scripture.

It's one more indication of how many people live under the delusion that because they have good feelings about God or Jesus, and sign a line on a survey, they really are born-again Christians. This is the ultimate delusion. You can be deluded about a lot of things, but to be deceived about whether you're a Christian affects your eternal destiny. We have multitudes of deceived people who are bouncing along on the Jesus bandwagon and thinking everything is swell. For them, judgment is going to be one big surprise.

## FALSE ASSURANCE

So many people who aren't saved think they are, and they're going to be shocked to learn otherwise when it's too late. Many times they're lulled into this state because they have a false doctrine of assurance. Somebody has told them that as long as they ask Jesus into their hearts, or pray this prayer, or perform this little ceremony, they're safely in the kingdom.

We can't take someone's initial positive response to the gospel as absolute assurance that they're saved; nor should we be too quick to dismiss a person's uncertainty or discourage self-examination. The Holy Spirit alone gives genuine assurance: "The Spirit Himself bears witness with our spirit that we are children of God" (Rom. 8:16). Don't usurp His role in someone's life. Don't let false assurance overrule His convicting work.

People can be deceived about their salvation if they fail at self-examination. They get into such a mind-set, one that says everything is grace and forgiveness, that they never really bother to face their sin. They hear somebody say, "You don't have to confess your sin, your sin's already forgiven! Don't worry about that. Just go on and live your life!" It is a kind of antinomianism, an attitude of being against or indifferent to the law of God.

The Lord brings us to His communion table over and over again in order that each professing Christian may examine himself. Second Corinthians 13:5 says, "Examine yourselves as to whether you are in the faith. Test yourselves. Do you not know yourselves, that Jesus Christ is in you?—unless indeed you are disqualified." You need to look at your sin and your motivation for doing what you do. Believe me, if you are genuinely saved, God will confirm that by His Spirit witnessing with your spirit. Raising your hand or walking the aisle has nothing to do with it.

### FIXATION AND FAIR EXCHANGE

Another thing that causes people to be under the delusion they're saved when they're not is a fixation on religious activity. They go to church, hear sermons, sing songs, read the Bible, go to a Bible study, take a class, and because they're all wrapped up in religious activity, the illusion becomes convincing that they are believers. Many in the church are not: they are tares among the wheat.

Still another idea that lulls people into deception is what I call the fair exchange. Whenever this deceived person sees something wrong in his life, instead of dealing directly with it and examining whether he is a true Christian, he finds something right with his life and makes a fair exchange. It is like swapping around Weight Watchers points. "Oh, I can't be that bad. I mean, look what I did over here!" And he is always trading off the negatives and the positives, so instead of evaluating his life honestly with integrity and saying, "If I'm a believer, should I be doing this?" he says, "Well, I know I do that, but look what else I do!" He makes a fair exchange and white-washes the deal.

The bottom line is this: looking beyond all of your false assurance, religious activity, or fair exchanges, do you live with a desire for obedience to the Word of God? Is that the goal you're striving for—not for the perfection of your life (which comes only in heaven)? And when you disobey it, as we all do daily, do you have a sense of conviction and remorse that draws you to confess it to God? If that isn't there, it's a fair question whether you're a Christian.

For example, I can't believe how many times I've talked with people in the homosexual movement who insist they're born-again Christians because they believe in Jesus, can recite their creed, tell you the date they were saved, and so forth. My answer to them is, "If you were Christians, you wouldn't sin continually, as you do, and defend it. You would be brokenhearted and repentant, and you would pray to have your life changed."

The world is filled with people who live as if they don't believe the Bible, but they insist they're Christians nonetheless. The fact is, they are unwilling to submit to the lordship of Christ as revealed in His Word, and that lack reveals that their claim to Christianity is a tragic illusion.

## THE DECEIVED

A lot of people are deluded about who really is a Christian. Apart from hypocrites, there are two categories of the deceived in the church: the superficial and the involved.

The superficial are the ones who call themselves Christians because, when they were little, they went to church or Sunday school, they got confirmed, or they "made a decision" for Christ. You may have heard someone, when he is getting baptized, say, "I received Christ when I was twelve, but my life was a mess after that, and now I want to get back to the faith." The truth probably is that he never received Christ at all when he was twelve. He went through some superficial religious activity and was deceived into thinking he was saved as a result.

The involved who are deceived are a much more subtle and serious group. They're immersed in the activities of the church, up to their necks. They know the gospel and biblical theology, but they don't obey the Word of God. They live in a constant state of sin.

How does a deceived person know he's deceived? And how can we spot such a person? Here are some keys, although not everybody doing these things will be deceived.

First, look for someone who's seeking feelings, blessings, experiences, healings, angels, and miracles. He is more interested in the by-products of the faith than the faith itself. He is more interested in what he can get than the glory God can get; more interested in himself than in the exaltation of Christ.

Second, look for people who are more committed to the denomination, the church, or the tradition than to the Word of God. Their kind of Christianity may be purely social. They're more committed to the organization than they are to the Lord and His Word.

Third, look for people who are involved in theology as an academic interest. You'll find them all over the colleges and seminaries of our land: people who study theology, write books on theology, and are absolutely void of any real righteousness. Theology, for them, is intellectual activity.

Fourth are people who always seem stuck on one overemphasized point of theology, like those who never teach on anything but the second coming of Christ in relation to current events. This is the person who bangs the drum constantly for his own little issue, point, or crazy quirk. He would like you to think that he is so close to God, he has a great divine insight no one else has, but the fact is, he is seeking a platform for feeding his ego. Watch for people with a lack of balance, and for those who are overindulgent in the name of grace, lacking penitence and a true contrite heart.

## A PERSONAL LESSON

Some of the most dramatic examples I've ever seen of the deceived disguised as Christians were people who had been my closest friends. The first was a high school classmate and teammate named Ralph. He and I worked summers at his dad's car dealership, repossessing cars from people who hadn't made their payments: a teenager's dream job. We spent a lot of other time together besides work and school, passing out tracts and witnessing in Pershing Square in downtown Los Angeles. He was the head of his church youth group, and I was the head of mine. He said all the right things and seemed for all the world to be on fire for Christ. But when he went off to college, he completely abandoned the faith. I was stunned.

In college I had a close friend named Don who was, I thought, a true spiritual friend in every sense. We were co-captains of the football team; he was class president and I was vice president; we both taught Bible studies; our dads were pastors, and we were thinking about being pastors too. We talked a lot together about serving the Lord. But then he went to Europe, got a Ph.D. in psychology, became a teacher and rock-concert promoter, and eventually was indicted, convicted, and sentenced for having students naked up in front of his classroom. He totally abandoned the faith.

Then I went to seminary, where one of my best friends, whose father was the dean, put a Buddhist altar in his house after he graduated. Here was someone who had prepared himself for a lifetime of teaching and preaching the truth of Scripture, yet whose whole life and ministry up to that time were revealed to be a deceptive lie.

These experiences were devastating, yet they showed me in an unforgettable way that somebody very involved in the church, saying all the right things, isn't always a Christian. Nothing else could have impressed the lesson on my heart more clearly. It kept sending me back to 1 John 2:19 for comfort and encouragement: "They went out from us, but they were not of us; for if they had been of us, they would have continued with us; but they went out that they might be made manifest, that none of them were of us."

## FAITH REQUIRES ACTION

Our main mission field in America today is within the church. We've got to get our own act together. Churches are loaded with people like my three former friends, who are filled with empty words. They say the right things at first, but they don't ultimately do God's will. We have to speak because the Bible tells us to confess, but confession without obedience is a sham. This is the case of the wise and foolish virgins in Matthew 25:1–3: "Then the kingdom of heaven shall be likened to ten virgins who took their lamps and went out to meet the bridegroom." The virgins here are symbolic of people who are attached to Christianity, and the bridegroom stands for Christ. "Now five of them were wise, and five were foolish," like the people who build on the rock and the sand. "Those who were foolish took their lamps and took no oil with them." In other words, they had a form of godliness, but they didn't have the power; they didn't have salvation in their hearts but just the trappings of it, the churchiness.

But the wise took oil in their vessels with their lamps. But while the bridegroom was delayed, they all slumbered and slept. And at midnight a cry was heard: "Behold, the bridegroom is coming; go out to meet him!" Then all those virgins arose and trimmed their lamps. And the foolish said to the wise, "Give us some of your oil, for our lamps are going out." But the wise answered, saying, "No, lest there should not be enough for us and you; but go rather to those who sell, and buy for yourselves." And while they went to buy, the bridegroom came, and those who were ready went in with him to the wedding, and the door was shut.

Afterward the other virgins came also, saying, "Lord, Lord, open to us!" But he answered and said, "Assuredly, I say to you, I do not know you." Watch therefore, for you know neither the day nor the hour in which the Son of Man is coming. (Matthew 25:4–13)

In verse 11, the foolish virgins were eager to confess, "Lord, Lord!" This is an interesting phrase. The first time they said, "Lord," it could have been from respect; the word means "master," "teacher," "sir." The second time, "Lord, Lord," may have emphasized the orthodoxy of their claim for the word "Lord." *Kurios* is the word translated in the Septuagint of the Old Testament for the name of Jehovah. They were saying, "We know You're God, we know You're Jehovah, we accept all that Your deity involves." They were respectful, they were orthodox, they used the right terms, they had the right attitudes, and using the word twice indicated their zeal and passion, their fervency, their commitment, and their strength of devotion. If the words of their profession meant anything, they would have met the basic condition of filling their lamps.

## LIVING RIGHTEOUSLY

Back in Matthew 7:22, as we saw earlier, Jesus quoted those who will appeal to get into the kingdom by repeating "in Your name" three times. In other words, "We're not so self-centered. We've been casting out demons for You, and we've been doing miracles for

You!" And we say, "These have got to be Christians." For some people, that claim will be legitimate, and the Lord will invite them into the kingdom.

But not every one who says that is going to enter, because not all who confess have been doing the will of the Father. In Matthew 7:23 the Lord made a confession, *homologeo*, of His own: "I never knew you." What a shock! He gave them a confession straight out of Psalm 6:8. They were banging on the door, saying, "Lord, Lord," and He responded, "Go away, I don't know you."

Of course He *knows* them; He knows everything. This isn't a matter of awareness or recognition. The word "know" in the Bible is used to characterize an intimate personal relationship. For example, in Amos 3:2, God said of Israel, "You only have I known of all the families of the earth." That doesn't mean the only people He knew about were Jews, but that He had an intimate relationship with just them.

The Old Testament says, "Cain knew his wife, and she bore a son" (see Gen. 4:17). That doesn't mean he knew who she was, or he knew her name; it means he knew her in the intimate act of marriage. When Mary was pregnant with our Lord, as the divine seed was infused by the Spirit of God, the Bible says Joseph was shocked because he had never "known her" (see Matt. 1:25).

Jesus sends away those who falsely claim to know Him because they "practice lawlessness" (Matt. 7:23). Instead of doing the will of God, and living by these righteous principles Jesus explained in the Sermon on the Mount, they live sinfully. It isn't what you *say* that proves the reality of your faith, it's what you *do*.

It means absolutely nothing to profess Christ if your life doesn't back it up. That's why Peter said that if you can't add virtue to your faith, you're not going to know if you're actually redeemed (see 2 Pet. 1:5–11?). That's what James meant when he said faith minus works equals zero (see James 2:17). The kind of "faith" that makes a verbal profession while the heart continues to pursue sin is no true faith at all. I think the epitome of taking the Lord's name in vain is not using His name as an expletive on the streets, but claiming Christ when He isn't yours.

G. Campbell Morgan wrote: "The blasphemy of the sanctuary is far more awful than the blasphemy of the slum." To say, "Lord, Lord," and then disobey is a Judas kiss. We must be heart-motivated and doing the will of God. That's why the Lord's Prayer says, "Thy will be done in earth as it is in heaven," which means our doing the Lord's heavenly will.

But what happens if you fail? We pray for forgiveness of our debts, or trespasses, "as we forgive those who trespass against us." Jesus wasn't saying, "Here's the perfect standard, and if you ever fail, you're out!" He was saying, "Here's the perfect standard, and part of the perfect standard is that when you fail, you deal with it." That's God's standard. And if these realities do not illustrate the direction of your life, I don't care what confession you've made, you're not a Christian.

## BIG TALK, LITTLE ACTION

True saving faith is a *repentant* faith in Jesus Christ, and that produces good works. If that's not there, it doesn't matter what you say. In my paraphrase of Matthew 7:23, the Lord says, "Not for one single moment have I acknowledged you as My own or known you intimately. You are forever expelled from My presence, because you continue to work lawlessness."

This is all the more astonishing because the claims in verse 22 are so impressive. These people have prophesied, cast out demons, done wonderful works—it sounds like much of what members of the charismatic movement claim today. Such claims are often not even true, much less valid grounds for the hope of heaven.

The point is that no matter what they claim, and no matter what miracles and wonders they've said they've done, Jesus says they are not qualified to be in His kingdom because they never came through the narrow gate. They didn't transform their words into actions.

We can't blame the Lord for condemning those who say but don't do, since, by their empty words, they show they have no place in His kingdom.

# 7

## THE ROCK OF TRUE FAITH

Where I live in southern California, we are constantly reminded of the need for a good foundation on a house. It seems as if we either have earthquakes or floods every year. Some years we had both at once. It was six o'clock in the morning, and a level 6.8 earthquake hit—that's a whopper. The doors started banging, the kids were flying out of a bed, and the radio newscaster reported that the dam above our house had broken and everybody had to evacuate. By God's providence, the only thing we lost was a shelf full of my athletic trophies. We went into the den and they were in a pile on the floor, the symbols of my long-ago gridiron glory, smashed to bits. (My wife used the opportunity to remind me that God blesses those who are humble. It's her favorite earthquake story.)

The climate in southern California is almost identical to the climate of Israel, and the people there are likewise no strangers to floods and the need for a sturdy foundation. It's dry and arid, for the most part, then when it rains, the land can absorb only so much, and the water becomes a flood. What may look like a wonderful, solid place to build a house in the summer becomes a raging torrent in winter that wipes out anything constructed there.

Jesus has this image in mind at the very end of the Sermon on the Mount, Matthew 7:24–27:

Therefore whoever hears these sayings of Mine, and does them, I
will liken him to a wise man who built his house on the rock: and
the rain descended, the floods came, and the winds blew and beat
on that house; and it did not fall, for it was founded on the rock.
But everyone who hears these sayings of Mine, and does not do
them, will be like a foolish man who built his house on the sand:
and the rain descended, the floods came, and the winds blew and
beat on that house; and it fell. And great was its fall.

These verses are the second closing statement of this sermon, after
verses 21–23, that contrast a right and a wrong response to the invitation of Christ.

Here Jesus pictured two men who built houses, probably in the
dry bed of a stream. One man worked feverishly on his house but
had absolutely no thought for the foundation; Jesus called him a
foolish man. The other man made sure he built his foundation upon
solid rock; Jesus called him a wise man. It's a widely known story.

But what seems a very simple parable is in fact a startling, powerful commentary on people who have head knowledge but empty
hearts. Notice that Jesus said in verse 24, "whoever hears" and in
verse 26, "everyone who hears." This refers to people who hear the
message, listen, and understand. They know what they're supposed
to do.

## MAN'S SPIRITUAL VALUES

Remember this is the Judge of the universe telling us how to build.
Unless you build your life on the foundation of divine righteousness,
you're going to be ruined. No matter what it looks like on the outside, no matter what you know in your head, no matter how feverishly you conduct your spiritual activity, if all you have is head
knowledge, you're going to get washed away when the flood comes.

The Jews had developed their own system of works, a self-serving effort of the flesh that fell far short, and God came along in Jesus, offering them true righteousness. But before they could receive it, they had to admit the bankruptcy of their own system. Jesus had been systematically tearing down their paper palace, piece by piece, throughout the Sermon on the Mount; by the time He got to Matthew 7, He had utterly destroyed their whole religious security. He forced them first to choose between the wide and the narrow gates, then to identify themselves with two builders who hear, one who obeys and one who doesn't.

Both builders represent people today who probably consider themselves Christians. Both of them may read Scripture, attend meetings at church, and be busy framing some kind of spiritual value system. The tremendous difference is that one is wise and one is a fool, because one builds on rock and the other builds on sand.

The foundation of a house is invisible. Once the building is finished, you can't see it anymore, so it becomes difficult to tell which home is solid and which isn't. Both houses look the same. Many people hear, but if you examine your life and it's all hearing and no doing, don't deceive yourself into thinking you're a Christian.

## SIDE BY SIDE

Several interesting similarities exist between the two builders in this parable. First of all, they both built houses, representing spiritual structures, so they were both involved in living their lives with the priority of spiritual activity that had to do with the kingdom of God.

Second, they probably built their houses in the same place, because the same storm hit them. True believers and false believers invariably live side by side; they're on the same block, they may attend the same church, they may listen to the same preacher, go to the same Bible studies, and be so similar they are indistinguishable to most people.

Third, they apparently built their houses with similar outward style because the only difference the Lord mentioned was the foundation. Both people may carry a Bible and a notebook, pray prayers, and take part in church activities. They may give similar amounts of money to the Lord. They both look like Christians until you come to the real crux of the matter, and that's the invisible foundation down at the bottom of everything. And only an honest and careful, soul-searching self-examination can reveal the truth concerning that hidden reality.

Jesus was trying to get the Pharisees to come off of their proud, high tower and see the spiritual bankruptcy in their own lives. The Pharisees had no regard for spirituality of soul, purity of heart, integrity of behavior, or obedience to God, and they were building their big spiritual structure on sand. Sure, they prayed and fasted and gave alms, but they did so only to impress God, to parade their supposed spirituality, and to enhance their reputations. They had a religion of externals; that is a religion of sand.

As Arthur Pink says,

They bring their bodies to the house of prayer, but not their souls; they worship with their mouths, but not "in spirit and in truth." They are sticklers for immersion or early morning communion, yet take no thought about keeping their hearts with all diligence. They boast of their orthodoxy, but disregard the precepts of Christ. Multitudes of professing Christians abstain from external acts of violence, yet hesitate not to rob their neighbours of a good name by spreading evil reports against them. They contribute regularly to the "pastor's salary," but shrink not from misrepresenting their goods and cheating their customers, persuading themselves that "business is business." They have more regard for the laws of man than those of God, for *His* fear is not before their eyes.[1]

## THE ROCK OF TRUE FAITH

The broad way that leads to destruction is all sand. The narrow roaders build on rock. What exactly does that mean? We could make a case for the fact that the rock is God, and you are literally building your life on God, which, of course, is true. We could say the rock is God, but so would the Pharisees. Or we could say the rock is Christ. Peter called Him the chief cornerstone (1 Pet. 2:6). Paul said He is the Rock (1 Cor. 10:4).

But plenty of people say they've built their lives on Christ. Most commentators say "rock" in this passage means God or Christ, but I want to take it a step further. Jesus is interested in "whoever hears these sayings of Mine, and does them." The rock is *true faith in the Word of God,* resulting in an obedient heart and the end of self-righteousness. Yes, God is a rock, yes, Christ is the chief cornerstone. But I believe that what our Lord was saying here is simply this: "These sayings of Mine become the bedrock foundation of the true church, the redeemed church, the true believer."

Look at Matthew 16:13–16: "When Jesus came into the region of Caesarea Philippi, He asked His disciples, saying, 'Who do men say that I, the Son of Man, am?'" And the answer was, "Some say John the Baptist, some Elijah, and others Jeremiah or one of the prophets." But Simon Peter answered, "You are the Christ, the Son of the Living God."

Jesus acknowledged this as a revelation, saying, "Flesh and blood has not revealed this to you, but My Father who is in heaven" (v. 17). That is a divine revelation. "And I also say to you that you are Peter"—*petros,* you are a boulder, a rock—"and on this rock"—*petra,* bedrock foundation—"I will build My church" (v. 18). And what was the *petra*, the bedrock of Christianity? It was the Word of God, the Christ, the Son of the living God. The *petra* of Matthew 16 was the Word of God, and I am convinced that the *petra* of Matthew 7 is the Word of God as well.

In Acts 20:32, Paul said, "I commend you . . . to the word of His grace, which is able to build you up." It is the Word of God that is our foundation, and it is the Word of God that provides the material for the building as well.

So, our Lord was saying that the person who lives a life in which he only *hears* and never *does* is living on the sand of human will, human opinion, human attitudes: the shifting sands of man's self-serving philosophy. Even though you listen, you're not on the rock. On the other hand, the wise man who hears the Word of God and builds his life on God's Word has a rock foundation. His heart has bowed in true faith and submission to the Word of God. And that bears the fruit of obedience.

John 8:30–32: "As He spoke these words, many believed in Him. Then Jesus said to those Jews who believed Him, 'If you abide in My word, you are My disciples indeed. And you shall know the truth, and the truth shall make you free.'" They heard, they truly believed, they accepted, they obeyed. That is building your life on the rock.

In James 1:22, we read this verse: "But be doers of the word, and not hearers only, deceiving yourselves." If you hear Jesus' Sermon on the Mount but don't do it, you're self-deceived; not because I say so, but because the Lord and His disciples say so. First John 2:3: "Now by this we know that we know Him, if we keep His commandments."

When you look at your life, do you see a heart that longs beyond any other desire to obey the Word of God? Or is it disobeying and always justifying that disobedience? *Obedience* is the key word. The only visible evidence you will ever have of your salvation is a life lived in the direction of obedience; it is the proof that you genuinely have bowed to the lordship of Jesus Christ and been transformed by His grace into a servant of His righteousness.

Sometimes God has to shock us into obedience by knocking us off our foundations. Possibly the only good thing about earthquakes in our California community is that they drive people to Christ. Rich or poor, famous or anonymous, they are petrified by their inability to control even the ground on which they walk. They come face-to-face with their powerlessness over the Creator Lord. Church attendance always goes up after a big quake, and in every case we see individuals, families, and couples come to Christ. Of course, some merely go through the motions, but for others it's the final push they need to repent before God's power.

## DEFINING THE DIFFERENCES

I saw an article in a magazine recently that asked, "What are pastors going to do with the new wave of unmarried Christians who are living together?" I question whether that can be true among Christians. Before we get concerned about who's living together, we had better be concerned about who's really a Christian. If these truths in the Sermon on the Mount don't define the direction of your life, then you are deluding yourself into thinking you're a Christian.

We've seen the similarities between the wise and foolish men, so now let's consider the differences. One built the easy way, the other built the hard way. It's easy to build on sand: just smooth out your spot and build a house. A fool does it the easy way for two reasons. First, fools are always in a hurry. Proverbs tells us that fools make haste. The fool is always looking for quick results, including quick evangelism: "Keep it moving, man, jump on the bandwagon, 'cause we're not slowing down!" No time for teaching the doctrine of sin, no time for building a sense of conviction, no time for coming to grips with your soul's condition before God. No time for developing a fear of divine judgment and eternal punishment. It's shortcut evangelism.

Second, the fool is superficial. He's one of those who proclaim they believe in Christ, who say they heard the gospel and accepted it, yet give no evidence of that by the way they live their lives. We live in the age of superficiality. Millions name the name of Jesus, but theirs is a shallow allegiance, unsteady like the shifting sand. And when they don't get their instant upper from Jesus anymore, don't get the jollies they were expecting, their house begins to collapse.

There's no deep plowing, no spadework, no foundation, no brokenness of heart in the foolish man. I think Spurgeon had a valuable word for us all when he said:

> Want of depth, want of sincerity, want of reality in religion—this is the want of our times. Want of an eye to God in religion, lack of sincere dealing with one's own soul, neglect of using the lancet with our hearts, neglect of the search warrant which God gives out against sin, carelessness concerning living upon Christ; much reading about him, much talking about him but too little feeding upon his flesh, and drinking of his blood—these are the causes of tottering professions and baseless hopes.[2]

## TAKING TIME TO DIG DEEP

While the foolish man is in a big hurry, the wise man takes time to do the job right. In the parallel passage to the end of Matthew 7, Luke 6:47–48 adds the fact that the wise man dug deep. He went for the rock of the Word of God. He blew the sand of human opinion and self-will away and fastened onto the bedrock of obedience to God's Word.

You can't dig deep if you're in a hurry. You just barely have time for a quickie conversion or lightweight confession. Some people say they are saved before they have any sense that they're even lost. Those who claim Christ legitimately as their own are willing to take time to dig deep. They've thought it through, they've counted the cost. Their profession of faith will not be rejected at the final judgment.

Remember in chapter 1, we looked at Luke 9:58–60, which tells us: "And Jesus said to him, 'Foxes have holes and birds of the air have nests, but the Son of Man has nowhere to lay His head.' Then He said to another, 'Follow Me.' But he said, 'Lord, let me first go and bury my father.'" What's interesting about that is his father wasn't even dead. He was actually thinking, "Let me go home and wait for the inheritance, then, soon as I get my money, I'm coming." "Jesus said to him, 'Let the dead bury their own dead, but you go and preach the kingdom of God.'" He was saying, "You let the world take care of its own; you come and preach the kingdom."

"And another also said, 'Lord, I will follow You, but let me first go and bid them farewell who are at my house.' But Jesus said to him, 'No one, having put his hand to the plow, and looking back, is fit for the kingdom of God'" (Luke 9:61–62). Those who come rushing in, but who want out again as soon as you start to lay down the standard for following Christ, are not fit for the kingdom.

## MAXIMUM EFFORT

Those who dig deep show a desire to give a maximum effort. The easy path always tempts us. Sometimes we make the gospel so easy that it's no gospel at all. We Christians stew about how hard it is to follow up with new converts. One large church in America reported it had 28,000 conversions in a year, baptized 9,600 people, and had 123 join the church. The fact is that 28,000 people weren't saved if only 123 joined the church. The problem is not the difficulty of follow-up; the problem is the difficulty of conversion. We're trying to follow up with people who never were redeemed.

I remember an "evangelism in depth" effort in Ecuador some years ago. The report was that thousands were saved, but only two could be found in a church. Those weren't conversions. True believers long, like babies, for the milk of the Word and Christian worship and fellowship. They love the Lord and His People.

Another characteristic of the man who digs deep is that he's teachable. The Pharisees weren't teachable; you couldn't tell them anything. So many people are like that; they profess Christ but don't want to hear all that true Christianity demands. The call to self-denial, they reject. They hold high their own ideas, goals, and designs. They want to go their way, and when you try to teach the right way instead, they don't want to hear it. It's not because they're unteachable Christians; it's because they're sham Christians.

The one who digs deep empties himself of self-righteousness and self-sufficiency, casts aside his own visions and experiences, and builds on the Word of God for God's glory and not his own.

## SATAN'S ULTIMATE WEAPON

One day, the truth of your faith or the evil of your deception will be revealed. The Chief Winnower is going to come to separate the wheat from the chaff. He's going to blow the wind of judgment, and those who have built their lives on the rock will stand. Revelation 20:12–15 specifically describes how it's going to happen:

> And I saw the dead, small and great, standing before God, and books were opened. And another book was opened, which is the Book of Life. And the dead were judged according to their works, by the things which were written in the books. The sea gave up the dead who were in it, and Death and Hades delivered up the

dead who were in them. And they were judged, each one according to his works. Then Death and Hades were cast into the lake of fire. This is the second death. And anyone not found written in the Book of Life was cast into the lake of fire.

This is the Great White Throne judgment, where God finally and forever separates the true from the false. And I believe that is a day when there will be echoing through the corridors of that judgment hall "Lord! Lord!" And echoing back will come the reverberation of His reply, "Depart from Me, I never knew you!"

You may be respectful of Christ; you may be fervent and active in private devotion; you may be busy with public proclamation and spiritual activity; you may be building a religious life in the same community with true believers; and your little religious house may look exactly like theirs. But when the judgment comes, your house will be devastated if it's built on the sand of your own way rather than the rock of obedience to His Word. Make sure you have built your spiritual foundation on Christ and the solid rock of obedience to His Word.

## FINAL WARNING

Every presentation of the gospel must end with a warning of doom to the one who rejects it. Mere saying and hearing are no proof that a person's faith is authentic; real faith is visible in the one who *does*.

There are times when all of us will stumble into a sin, but if unrepentant sin is the pattern of your life, you're not in His kingdom. See if you're in this list from 1 Corinthians 6:9–10: "Do you not know that the unrighteous will not enter the kingdom of God? Do not be deceived. Neither fornicators, nor idolaters, nor adulterers, nor homosexuals, nor sodomites, nor thieves, nor coveters, nor drunkards, nor revilers, nor extortioners will inherit the kingdom of God."

If you're not on that list, look at the one in Galatians 5:19–21: "adultery, fornication, uncleanness, lewdness, idolatry, sorcery, hatred, contentions, jealousies, outbursts of wrath, selfish ambitions, dissensions, heresies, envy, murders, drunkenness, revelries, and the like . . . those who practice such things will not inherit the kingdom of God."

And there are plenty more lists of human sins that keep people out of heaven. Who gets in, then? The few who truly repent of their sins; the few who find the narrow gate.

When you eagerly give your life in submission to the Lord, He takes over and everything begins to unfold, and from there on He begins to empower and change you. C. S. Lewis has a marvelous illustration of this:

> When I was a child I often had a toothache, and I knew that if I went to my mother she would give me something which would deaden the pain for that night and let me get sleep. But I did not go to my mother—at least, not till the pain became very bad. And the reason I did not go was this. I did not doubt she would give me the aspirin; but I knew she would also do something else. I knew she would take me to the dentist next morning. I could not get what I wanted out of her without getting something more, which I did not want. I wanted immediate relief from pain; but I could not get it without having my teeth set permanently right. And I knew those dentists; I knew they started fiddling about with all sorts of other teeth which had not yet begun to ache. They would not let sleeping dogs lie.[3]

Our Lord is like that dentist. If you give Him one problem to fix, He'll fix them all. That's why He warned people to count the cost before becoming Christians. He will make you perfect—nothing less. That process begins the moment you trust Him and continues until the moment you arrive in heaven and are instantly glorified. When you put yourself in His hands, that's what you're in for, whatever it takes.

# 8

## HALLMARKS OF DISCIPLESHIP

Theodore Roosevelt once said, "There has never yet been a man who led a life of ease, whose name is worth remembering." Certainly when the Lord calls us to be His disciples, He does not call us to a life of ease.

A missionary whose story has influenced my life greatly is a man mentioned earlier named Henry Martyn. After a long and difficult life of Christian service in India, he announced he was going to go to Persia (modern Iran), because God had laid it upon his heart to translate the New Testament and the Psalms into the Persian language.

By then he was an old man. People told him that if he stayed in India, he would die from the heat, and that Persia was hotter than India. But he went nonetheless. There he studied the Persian language and then translated the entire New Testament and Psalms in nine months. Then he learned that he couldn't print or circulate them until he received the Shah's permission. He traveled six hundred miles to Tehran; there he was denied permission to see the Shah. He turned around and made a four-hundred-mile trip to find the British ambassador, who gave him the proper letters of introduction and sent him the four hundred miles back to Tehran. This was in 1812, and Martyn made the whole trip on the back of a mule, traveling at night and resting by day, protected from the sweltering desert sun by nothing but a strip of canvas.

He finally arrived back in Tehran, was received by the Shah, and secured permission for the Scriptures to be printed and circulated in Persia. Ten days later he died. But shortly before his death, he had written this statement in his diary: "I sat in the orchard, and thought, with sweet comfort and peace, of my God; in solitude my Company, my Friend, and Comforter."

He certainly did not live a life of ease, but it was a life worth remembering. And he's one of many God used to turn redemptive history.

Bound up in the spirit of Henry Martyn is the key to genuine discipleship, which is to be so utterly consumed with the cause that you have no thought for your own life. Verses 38–39 of Matthew 10 highlight this aspect of serving Christ: "And he who does not take his cross and follow after Me is not worthy of Me. He who finds his life will lose it, and he who loses his life for My sake will find it."

Many people claim to follow Jesus. Many people claim to be His disciples, and many always have. But in these verses of Matthew, our Lord pointed to the proof of genuineness. This is the mark of a real follower of Christ.

The message of genuineness is one the Lord spoke about again and again. But it seems to be one that today's Christian church often overlooks. The Lord repeatedly compared true disciples against false, the real against the fake. For Him, this was an essential matter. And so He talked frequently about genuine salvation as opposed to a facade of salvation.

In Matthew alone, this is a constant issue. In chapter 5, verse 20, His first sermon recorded in the New Testament, our Lord said this: "For I say to you, that unless your righteousness exceeds the righteousness of the scribes and Pharisees, you will by no means enter the kingdom of heaven." There is the genuine, perfect righteousness of Christ that is imputed to each believer (Rom. 4:5; Phil. 3:9; 2 Cor. 5:21), and there is a false righteousness of men. And unless you have the real thing, you'll not enter the kingdom. Jesus was focusing here on the sham righteousness of the Pharisees.

We have seen the same warning in Matthew 7, where Jesus spoke of that narrow gate that only a few people ever find. There are two roads that seem to go to God, but one leads to life, the other to destruction. Later in that same sermon, Jesus concluded with the parable of the man who built his house on sinking sand while his neighbor built on solid rock.

The Lord began Matthew 13 with a discussion of a sower and seed. In verses 4–8, the sower cast his seeds with these results:

> Some seed fell by the wayside; and the birds came and devoured them. Some fell on stony places, where they did not have much earth; and they immediately sprang up because they had no depth of earth. But when the sun was up they were scorched, and because they had no root they withered away. And some fell among thorns, and the thorns sprang up and choked them. But others fell on good ground and yielded a crop: some a hundredfold, some sixty, some thirty.

This story tells us that in response to the preaching of the gospel, there are at least four different possible results. And only one of them is genuine reception, producing righteousness.

The lesson appears once more, beginning in Matthew 13:47–50:

> "Again, the kingdom of heaven is like a dragnet that was cast into the sea and gathered some of every kind, which, when it was full, they drew to shore; and they sat down and gathered the good into vessels, but threw the bad away. So it will be at the end of the age.

The angels will come forth, separate the wicked from among the just, and cast them into the furnace of fire. There will be wailing and gnashing of teeth."

The church is a net that pulls in every kind of person, good and bad. And one day, angels will separate the true followers from the false. Time and again in the New Testament, the Lord brought up the idea of identifying the true disciples as well as the pretenders. So Matthew 10:38–39 is consistent with the message as it occurs throughout Scripture.

I'm notorious in some circles for being "too inflexible" in defining what does and does not characterize a true follower of Christ. Here's the only truth: the supreme authority of God's revelations in Scripture. Nothing else counts. This deep loyalty to the truth I absorbed to a large extent from Dr. Charles Fineberg, a converted Jew, an immense intellect, and the dean of Talbot Seminary, where I graduated. He was my mentor, had a high view of Scripture, and taught me to have the same.

Even more so, my father taught me the truth of Scripture. He was a great teacher and a Bible expositor, one who allows the Word of God to frame his understanding of salvation. He got the story straight and preached it right. He is ninety years old and still does. His radio ministry is in its sixty-third year; he also writes a monthly newsletter and teaches Sunday school every week. There was never anything shallow about his ministry. And he taught me there's never any doubt about what makes true salvation and discipleship.

## ACTION AND REACTION

The apostle Paul made a paradoxical statement in Romans 9:6 when he said, "All Israel is not Israel." In other words, all who are outwardly Jews are not inwardly Jews. All who are outwardly identified as the people of God are not inwardly the people of God. And we could say, then, that all disciples are not disciples; all apparent followers of Jesus are not actual followers of Jesus. We could even say that all the church, as we see it, is not the church.

Matthew 10 describes the hallmarks of a genuine disciple. The message there is a message, first of all, about genuineness, and second, a message about impact: Who is a real disciple? How does he impact the world? How does the world impact him?

The first characteristic of a genuine disciple is that he is like his Lord. He bears the character of Christ. That's why in Acts 11:26 people called the believers Christians: *Christiani*—"iani" means "belonging to the party of." They were little Christs; they manifested His character and bore the marks of His life in them. A true Christian not only wears the name of Christ, but he demonstrates the virtue of Christ. Matthew 10:24–25 declares a self-evident axiom: "A disciple is not above his teacher, nor a servant above his master. It is enough for a disciple that he be like his teacher, and a servant like his master." People become like those whose influence dominates them.

Jesus repeated this truism in Luke 6:40, saying, "A disciple is not above his teacher, but everyone who is perfectly trained will be like his teacher." Beyond the discipling of the Spirit of Christ in us is the reality that He Himself has come to live in us, so that we can say with Paul, "It is no longer I who live, but Christ lives in me" (Gal. 2:20). A true disciple acts like Christ. Of course, there'll be lapses because of our humanness, but nonetheless there will be evidence of Christlikeness in the life of a true believer.

If we're true disciples, we have Jesus' hallmark on us; He is our maker. He is our life. Paul wonderfully affirmed this in 2 Corinthians 5:17: "Therefore, if anyone is in Christ, he is a new creation; old things have passed away; behold, all things have become new." That newness must be manifest.

The second and consequential characteristic of true disciples is that if we are like Christ, other people will respond to us as they did Christ. Matthew 10:25 continues: "If they have called the master of the house Beelzebub, how much more will they call those of his household!" Being a genuine Christian means to exhibit the character of Christ and, thus, to be treated as He was treated. When we move into the world with Christlike character, the world will react to us the way it reacted to Him. That was Jesus' message in John 15:20 when He said, "'A servant [some translations read "slave"] is not greater than his master.' If they persecuted Me, they will also persecute you. If they kept [obeyed] My word, they will keep yours also."

If you are genuine in your identification with Christ, you can expect the world that rejects Christ to reject you.

## FEAR AND FAVOR

Still, it is also characteristic of a true disciple of Jesus that he is not afraid of the world. Matthew 10:28: "And do not fear those who kill the body but cannot kill the soul. But rather fear Him who is able to destroy both soul and body in hell." There's no reason to be afraid, because, as a follower of Jesus, you know you will happily trade whatever perils you face in this world for the riches of your reward in the eternal world to come. Disciples joyfully "speak in the light" and "preach on the housetops" (v. 27), untroubled by any rebuke or threat. Furthermore, there's no reason to fear what happens here, because not even a sparrow falls (actually the word means "hops") to the ground outside of God's will. "But the very hairs of your head are all numbered. Do not fear therefore; you are of more value than many sparrows" (vv. 30–31).

When the world is hostile and persecuting, when the world moves against him and ostracizes or alienates him, a true disciple is not afraid, because he has utterly and totally given himself over to the lordship of Christ, confident in His care no matter what, even against the hostility of the world.

Another characteristic of discipleship is that a true disciple is loyal to his Lord. In verse 32 Jesus told us, "Therefore whoever confesses Me before men, him I will also confess before My Father who is in heaven." When the heat is on, when the pressure and the persecution are bearing down and the world is attacking, the true believer will openly confess Christ. He won't bail out. He won't deny his faith. He won't recant. He'll stand up and proclaim Christ, no matter what the circumstances. He'll go to prison and even face execution before he will deny his Lord.

Someone will say, "What about Peter? He was a real disciple, but he denied his Lord." It's true. He did. But it was before the Holy Spirit came to live in him. After that, he never again was disloyal. He died for being loyal to Christ: crucified upside down, as he requested, because he said he was not worthy to die like his Lord. Such loyalty marks the ones whom Christ will confess belong to Him.

## THE SWORD OF CHRIST

A central characteristic of a true disciple—and in some ways, almost an unbelievable one, because it goes so radically against our natural longings—is a willingness to forsake family if necessary. In Matthew 10:34, which we looked at earlier, Jesus said: "Do not think that I came to bring peace on earth. I did not come to bring peace but a sword." This is a most dramatic statement. He was saying, "Now, some of you who are real will confess Me when you're brought to the tribunals and the courts of men, and even in the course of day-to-day life. Others of you will deny Me, because it isn't that important to you, and you'll save your necks and your reputations. And that just proves that I have come to bring a sword. I cause divisions. I force people to decisions that separate one from another." The very fact that some confess Christ and some deny Christ indicates that His coming causes divisions. Jesus didn't deny that stark reality, He built on it.

The Jews knew from the Old Testament that when the Messiah came, He was coming to bring peace. Isaiah prophesied that He would be the Prince of Peace (9:6). Under His reign, warring factions would beat their swords into plowshares and their spears into pruning hooks (Isa. 2:4). War—even the knowledge of war—would pass away.

They knew the marvelous words of hope in Psalm 72:3, 7 as it talks of the kingdom: "The mountains will bring peace to the people . . . / . . . In His days the righteous shall flourish, / And abundance of peace, / Until the moon is no more." There would be no war, only peace.

As Jesus was speaking to the disciples, they had already begun to experience the peace in their hearts that came just from being with Him. And they may have been anticipating that this bliss would extend to everybody. The disciples may have imagined they would go out to preach, and the whole world would fall at their feet because the Messiah, the Prince of Peace they had awaited for so long, had finally arrived. They were experiencing this euphoria of being with Him, confident that everybody else would respond the same way and Christ's wonderful, peaceful kingdom was just around the corner.

But that wasn't the true picture. So the Lord told them, "Don't be under any illusions about My coming now to bring peace. I've come not to send peace, but a sword." This idea expressed here sounds as if the Lord's intention for coming was to bring conflict. Consequences are often expressed as if they were intentions, for in the ultimate sovereignty of God, they are. But here, Jesus described the direct result of His coming as if it were His deliberate intention. And this is a paradox, in a sense. The Lord was saying, "On the one hand, I'm a prince of peace, but on the other hand, there's going to be war, represented by a sword."

The Old Testament represented both of these points of view. It saw the fracturing, the breaking asunder. Micah 7:6 describes the Lord's coming this way: "For son dishonors father, / Daughter rises against her mother, / Daughter-in-law against her mother-in-law; / A man's enemies are the men of his own household." Our Lord almost directly quoted that in Matthew 10.

The Old Testament saw the Messiah as a king of peace, but it also saw a potential for division in His coming because some would accept Him, and others, even in the same family, would reject Him. The Jews also believed this division would take place. In some of the rabbinical writings, we find this statement: "In the period when the Son of David shall come, a daughter will rise up against her mother, a daughter-in-law against her mother-in-law. The son despises his father, the daughter rebels against the mother, the daughter-in-law against the mother-in-law, and a man's enemies are they of his own household."

It's as if Jesus was saying there will be a division *for the moment*. The intervention of God in history through the incarnation of Christ was going to split and fracture the world into parties that would pit themselves against one another. So don't be under any illusion as a disciple to think the whole world is going to fall at your feet. You're going to rush home and tell everybody you've become a Christian? You're going to shout the news at school, and everybody's going to line up to join you? It's not going to happen.

## THE BIGGEST RIFT

Martin Luther said, "If our gospel were received in peace, it wouldn't be the true gospel." If anybody ever saw the truth of Christianity divide people and institutions, it was Luther. He preached the truth in the Catholic church, but it didn't bring peace; it created the biggest rift in the history of religion. It shattered the monolithic power of the

Catholic hierarchy and gave birth to the Protestant Reformation, which rescued the true gospel from its sacramental captor.

In a real sense, Matthew 10:34 is paradoxical because we should expect the Lord to bring peace. After all, John the Baptist was His herald, and he talked about peace. When the angels proclaimed His birth, they said, "Peace on earth." And Jesus, in John 14:27, said, "My peace I give to you."

In at least three places in the book of Romans, Paul talked about the peace that God has given us (5:1, 8:6, 14:17). It's true that there is peace in the heart of the one who believes, but as far as the world is concerned, there's nothing but division. Yes, He brought the peace of God to the heart of a believer, and someday there will be a kingdom of peace. The Old Testament didn't always make a clear distinction between the First Coming and the Second Coming. The first brought a sword; the second will bring the ultimate peace.

It is true that the First Coming brought a partial peace, the peace that enters the hearts of those who believe. But the Lord warned the disciples, "You just remember this as you go out: You're going to cause division. You're going to cause a rending and a splitting apart."

The gospel does that. It is the refiner's fire that consumes. It brings the shepherd's separation of the sheep and the goats. It brings the husbandman's fan when he throws the grain into the air and the chaff is blown away. The entrance of Christ splits and tears apart. If Christ had never come, the earth would have gone on in unity, doomed to hell. But when He came, a war broke out.

In Luke 12 we see something of this. In verse 49, Jesus said, "I came to send fire on the earth, and how I wish it were already kindled!" Verse 51: "Do you suppose that I came to give peace on earth? I tell you, not at all, but rather division." He came to bring a sword, not peace, in the sense that He came to set members of a family against each other. He was saying that if you're a true disciple, you'll be willing to create a division in your own home.

That goes against all of our instincts because we want peace in our homes more than anywhere else. That's our refuge, that's where the people we love the most and know the best live. We don't want to be at odds with them. But when we commit ourselves to Jesus Christ, we'll be true to Him, even if it destroys our homes, our neighborhoods, our cities, or our nation. If that's the price, we'll pay it.

Jesus expressed the severity of this severance in the phrase in Matthew 10:35: "For I have come to set a man against his father." Some translations have "set a man at variance against his own father." The Greek term for "at variance" or "set against" is a rare one, used only here in the New Testament. It means to cut asunder. Jesus was saying, "I will cut a man off totally from his father, and all these other relatives from each other. I'll fracture families every way possible."

This is the worst rending that can happen. It's not so bad when you're at odds with your neighbor, your boss, your friend, or your society, but when it gets into the family, and your commitment to Jesus Christ means that you are severed from your relatives, that's where it really begins to rub. Your commitment to Christ goes against your love and need for them.

Your commitment goes against the harmony with which you desire to live. Being a Christian and following Jesus Christ may mean you create a division in your own home. But that's the mark of a true disciple. Clinging to Christ often means letting go of family members who reject you because you won't reject the gospel. That's especially true in Jewish families, as well as those in false religions.

This is a hard standard, and many people decide it's too much of a sacrifice. Some wives will not come to Christ for fear of separation from their husbands. Some husbands will not come to Christ for fear of separation from their wives. Children may not come to Christ for fear of their fathers or mothers, and vice versa. People will not take a stand for Christ, because they want to maintain that family harmony. But Jesus said the true disciple will turn from his family, if he is forced to make a choice. This is part of self-denial, accepting gladly the high cost of following Jesus to receive His infinite blessings for time and eternity.

## A HIGHER LOVE

Family love is strong, surely the tightest human bond. But it doesn't have the power that love for Christ has. It is so strong that it sometimes cuts the family bond. One young lady I know said she had become a Christian from a totally pagan family and, as a result, her father, whom she greatly loved, refused to speak to her either in person or on the phone; he would hang up on her. She said, "I would think he'd be happy that I'm not an alcoholic, I'm not a drug addict, I'm not a criminal, and that I haven't been in some terrible accident, crippled, or injured. I've never had such joy in my life as I have now as a Christian, and because of my love for Christ he won't talk to me." That's because of the sword.

The same sword fell between Cain and Abel. Abel was a righteous man, Cain was an unrighteous man, and the cleavage was so great that Cain couldn't stand it—so he murdered his brother.

First Corinthians 7 tells us how that sword comes right into a Christian marriage. If you have an unbelieving wife, and she wants to stay with you, don't divorce her. If you have an unbelieving husband who wants to stay with you, then let him stay, because a certain sanctifying occurs. That is, the blessing that falls on the believer from God splashes onto the unbelieving partner in a temporal way. "But if the unbeliever departs, let him depart; a brother or sister is not under bondage in such cases. But God has called us to peace" (v. 15). That's the other side of it. Once the sword falls, then God has called us to peace, and if the unbeliever wants out, let him out.

Becoming a Christian means being sick of your sin, longing for forgiveness and rescue from present evil and future hell, and affirming your commitment to the lordship of Christ to the point where you are willing to forsake everything. I've said it before and I'll say it again: it isn't just holding up your hand or walking down an aisle and saying, "I love Jesus." It is not easy, it is not user-friendly or seeker-sensitive; it isn't a rosy, perfect world where Jesus gives you whatever you want. It is hard, it is sacrificial, and it supersedes everything.

The manifestation of true faith is a commitment that no influence can sway. Of course you love your family, your children, your parents, and your husband or wife. But if you're a real disciple, your commitment to the salvation found only in Christ is so deep, profound, and far-reaching that you will say no, if need be, to those you love for the cause of Christ.

John Bunyan knew all about this in a special way. The authorities told John Bunyan to quit preaching, but he said, "I cannot quit preaching, because God has called me to preach." And they said, "If you preach, we'll put you in prison."

So he said to himself, "If I go to prison, who cares for my family? Yet how can I close my mouth when God has called me to preach?"

He was brave and faithful enough to commit his family to the care of God; he remained obedient to the call of God and preached, and they put him in prison. Then it was in prison that he wrote his magnificent allegory *The Pilgrim's Progress* that has blessed so many millions of families down through the centuries, with its teaching about the path to salvation. His family suffered without him, but God cared for them. And through that suffering, God accomplished mighty works in the lives of countless others.

Bunyan wrote in an appendix to his autobiography, *Grace Abounding to the Chief of Sinners,*

> The parting with my Wife and poor Children hath often been to me in this place [jail], as the pulling of the Flesh from my Bones; and that not only because I am somewhat too fond of these great

Mercies, but also because I should have often brought to my mind the many hardships, miseries, and wants that my poor Family was like to meet with, should I be taken from them, especially my poor blind Child, who lay nearer my heart than all I have besides. O the thought of the hardship I thought my blind one might go under, would break up my heart to pieces . . . But yet, recalling my self, thought I, I must venture you all with God, though it goeth to the quick to leave you; O I saw in this condition, I was a man who was pulling down his House upon the head of His wife and Children; yet thought I, I must do it, I must do it.[1]

I pray to God I never have to make that decision, but I might. You may have had to make that choice because you confessed Jesus Christ, and it has been a burden on your family. But that's the way we prove the reality of our conversion. The one who says, "I'm not willing to make that sacrifice" isn't genuine. "He who loves father or mother more than Me," said Jesus in Matthew 10:37, "is not worthy of Me." You can't be His disciple and receive His salvation if your family means more to you than He does.

## WILLING TO DIE

Only one thing is even more apt than the family to rob Christ of His rightful place in the heart of an individual, and that is the love of his own life. Sure, you might be willing to take Christ and lose your family, but would you be willing to take Christ and lose your life?

Now we're getting serious about who is a Christian.

Matthew 10:38: "And he who does not take his cross and follow after Me is not worthy of Me." We're back to that cross again. The whole point of this section of biblical text is to stress one incredible idea: total self-denial to the point of death.

The Lord was really zeroing in on what a true believer was.

Unless you're willing to take up your cross and follow Him, you aren't truly a follower. No doubt you've heard a zillion devotionals on "taking up your cross." But as we saw earlier in our look at Luke 9, your cross isn't your broken-down car or your unappreciative spouse. When Jesus told His listeners to take up their crosses, it meant only one thing to them. It meant willingly facing the possibility of death for His sake.

Eleven of the twelve apostles (all except Judas) were from Galilee, where another Judas, Judas of Galilee, had recently led an insurrection. He gathered a force to throw the Romans out, but the Romans won. They crushed Judas and his insurrection. The Roman general, Varus, wanting to teach the Jews a lesson, crucified more than two thousand of them. He put their crosses up and down all the roads of Galilee, so people saw them everywhere they traveled. Every crucified Jew had carried his own crossbeam as he marched to death by crucifixion.

These Galileans had seen all of that, and Jesus was talking to them in a historical context, saying they needed to be willing to face such a consequence rather than deny Him. Jesus was saying that to follow Him, we must be willing to go through the most horrific death imaginable.

Committing your life to follow Jesus Christ means you would not only forsake your family if need be, you'd give your life. The world should never intimidate you, and you must be willing to confess Christ in the most hostile environment.

The disciples understood that to "take up the cross" meant a willingness to die any death. It meant abandoning self to the lordship of Christ. The love of Christ has to overrule both the powerful appeal of family love and the more powerful instinct of self-preservation.

As we heard in other texts, again Jesus added this rich thought in Matthew 10:39: "He who finds his life will lose it, and he who loses his life for My sake will find it." Whoever protects his physical safety by denying Christ under pressure will lose his eternal soul. But if you're willing to lose your life for Christ's sake, you'll find eternal life in the end. Being a martyr doesn't save you. If you're a genuine Christian, though, you value nothing so much that you will turn away from Christ, knowing that the one who confesses Jesus Christ and dies for Him is far better off than the apostate who escapes death by denying Christ and receives eternal damnation.

Officials brought John Bunyan before the magistrates when they put him in prison, and he said, "Sir, the law of Christ hath provided two ways of obeying: The one to do that which I in my conscience do believe I am bound to do, actively; and where I cannot obey it actively, there I am willing to lie down and suffer what they shall do unto me."

He was right. If you serve Christ actively and aggressively, you pay the price. But it is better to lose everything here—better to lose your ease and comfort, to be hassled and intimidated, badgered by the world; better even to lose your family, to lose your life—than to forsake Jesus Christ. And thank God, it isn't that we will necessarily have to make all these sacrifices, but if we're really His, if it comes to that, we will do it. Salvation in Christ is that precious.

## THE JOY OF BELIEVING

These last two sections on persecution and suffering are also characteristics of a true believer. Seen in this light, the truth about being a disciple seems filled with sacrifice and foreboding. Does being a Christian mean you're destined to face the world's harassment, having to confess before men, forsaking your family, and giving your life? Don't we do anything but create problems in the world?

Of course we do. A true disciple receives his due reward. As well as creating war, strife, division, separation, and friction, we do have a positive effect. We are the destiny-determiners in the world. When we bring down the sword that separates, on the one hand are the unbelievers, but on the other hand are the *believers*. And when we preach, live, and give our testimonies, thank God some respond in genuine repentance and self-denying faith.

Everything is as bright for them as it is dark for the nonbelievers. Not everyone is going to refuse the message of the disciple. Some are going to believe and receive their Lord. And since we have limited ability to reward their faith, the Lord will do it for us.

Matthew 10:40: "He who receives you receives Me, and he who receives Me receives Him who sent Me." Let me tell you what's in the word "receive" here. When you represent Jesus Christ and proclaim His Word, the people who believe it are the ones who receive you. It is a full receiving, in that they accept you and your message. And the ones who receive you are also receiving the Lord. In turn, the ones receiving the Lord are receiving the one who sent the Lord. That means you become an agency of men's receiving God Himself. Wow! What greater privilege could we imagine?

On the one hand, you create this antagonism by standing fast in the faith, then, on the other hand, you create this marvelous reality that people receive God through you. Every time somebody says to me, "You know, I was saved when you preached," or "I received Christ when you told me the gospel," I am thrilled beyond the ability to express. I didn't save anybody, but God used me as His instrument to forgive and reconcile those people to Himself forever.

It's pretty overwhelming to grasp that God has used a frail, human, clay pot as His means of saving others. But the reward goes even beyond that. Look at Matthew 10:41: "He who receives a prophet in the name of a prophet shall receive a prophet's reward. And he who receives a righteous man in the name of a righteous man shall receive a righteous man's reward." That's a tremendous divine principle. By the way, a prophet is what he *says*, and a righteous man is what he *is*, so the two really speak of the same individual. A true disciple lives what he says. He speaks the gospel truth, and he lives righteously.

When you go out representing God by your life and your lips, by your speaking and your living, those who receive you will receive the reward that you receive. This could be true of a pastor, a teacher, a missionary, an evangelist, or anyone who represents Christ; the one who receives that one will share that one's reward. If the Lord gives me a reward for proclaiming to you, He'll give you the same reward for receiving what I proclaim. We all share.

You want to be a blessing in the world? Then confess Christ before men! Stand up boldly, and don't mitigate your testimony; don't be ashamed of Christ. Don't water down the truth. And let your life become the source of their reward. Then a disciple is a person who determines destiny. Even the least of us shares with the greatest of us in what God does in blessing us.

## BRIDGE BUILDERS

There was a lad in a country village, who, after a great struggle, reached the ministry. All through his days of study, a cobbler in the village had helped him. He was a simple man but well-read, and he loved God with all his heart.

In time, the young lad he had helped became licensed to preach, and on the day of his ordination, the cobbler said to him, "Young man, I always had in my heart the desire to be a minister of the gospel, but the circumstances of my life never made it possible. You are doing what was always my dream, but never reality. I want you to promise me one thing. I want you to let me make you a pair of shoes for nothing, and I want you to wear them in the pulpit when you preach. Then I'll feel you are preaching the gospel I always wanted to preach, standing in my shoes."

Because of whom he represents, you will receive a disciple no matter how meager or unassuming he is. And in that true receiving, you will receive the message he brings of the Savior and the Father, and you will embrace the whole of the blessedness of God's eternal gifts to those who are His own.

Being a disciple of Jesus Christ is pretty fantastic. You become the source of conflict for some of the world, and the source of blessing for others. But you and I who are the disciples of Christ, we draw the lines. I pray we'll always be willing to follow the lordship of Christ at any price, in order that some may be antagonized, and some may be blessed.

In the depths of winter, Napoleon's army was retreating from its invasion of Russia. The army was pressed on all sides and had to cross the Berezina River to escape. The Russians had destroyed all the bridges, and Napoleon ordered that a bridge be built across the river. The men nearest the water were the first to attempt to carry out the almost impossible task. Several were carried away by the furious rapids. Others drowned due to the cold and their exhaustion, but more came and the work proceeded as quickly as possible. Finally, the builders completed the bridge and emerged half-dead from the icy water. As a result of that incredible effort the French army marched across the Berezina River in safety.[2]

That was an instance of heroic self-sacrifice. in a similar way, Christ calls His disciples to give their lives to build bridges for others to cross into the presence of God. If you're a true disciple, you will be willing to do just that.

# 9

## CAN'T GET NO SATISFACTION

Some people in this world refuse to be satisfied. No doubt you've run into them at work, in your neighborhood, and even at church. It's always too stuffy in the room for them except when its too drafty. They're too busy except when they're bored to death; they always have too much responsibility or too little; and nothing is ever quite the way it ought to be, according to their way of thinking. As the song says, they "can't get no satisfaction."

Fault-finders have an easy target in Christianity. It's too exclusive, too unyielding, with too many hypocrites, too dependent on faith over experience. It requires too much sacrifice. It is simply too hard to believe. Scripture shows us that people who are determined to resist the truth of the gospel are impossible to please, no matter what they hear. Whatever way someone tells the story of Christ's redemption, they will turn from it because their hearts are shut tight.

We've seen the danger and futility of changing the message of Christianity to make it more popular and acceptable to such hard-headed people. Some out there are going to reject Christ, no matter how much biblical truth they hear.

One of the greatest examples in history begins with the rejection of John the Baptist when he proclaimed to Israel that the Messiah had arrived. His appearance, lifestyle, and teaching methods put off his listeners. But then, when Jesus Himself began His ministry using a contrasting and completely different approach, the same people rejected Him too. They refused to be satisfied with the message, no matter what the style of the messenger.

## UNCOMPROMISING GREATNESS

John the Baptist came from a common, humble family without any noteworthy education or social grace, and without any previous accomplishments to his credit. And yet our Lord said he was the greatest human being who ever lived up to that time. Matthew 11:11: "Assuredly, I say to you, among those born of women there has not risen one greater than John the Baptist; but he who is least in the kingdom of heaven is greater than he." Jesus even emphasized the fact by starting with "Assuredly," which means "truly," or "a fact beyond dispute." Jesus offered no qualification or opinion here, just a statement of fact: "John is the greatest human being ever." John was greater than Adam or Abraham. He was greater than Isaac, Jacob, and Joseph; greater than Moses, Joshua, David, and Solomon.

John's personal character marked his greatness. He was a man who could recognize, acknowledge, and overcome his limitations, which is always a hallmark of greatness. Every person is either a victim of his situation or a victor over it. Everybody has challenges, weaknesses, failings, infirmities, and problems. The question is whether or not you can overcome them. The great ones fight through, and John did that.

He was a man of humility who recognized his shortcomings. Pride is an illusion that curses greatness. The great are the ones who see their failings and work to overcome, not the ones who fancy themselves to be without weakness. And as long as you admit no weakness, you will never grow to your full strength. This was a rare gift in the ancient world; neither the Romans nor the Greeks even had a word in their vocabulary for humility.

When some began to doubt the greatness of John, Jesus pointed out to them that they had already responded to his strength of conviction. Matthew 11:7 says, "As they departed, Jesus began to say [sarcastically] to the multitudes concerning John: 'What did you go out to the wilderness to see? A reed shaken by the wind?'"

It's a deceptively simple question. John had announced the arrival of the Messiah, and then people doubted whether he was a reliable guy. Jesus reminded John's listeners of their own attitude and experience with him. He was asking, "Why did you leave Galilee and make such a long, hard journey, all the way out to the desert around the Dead Sea? What was it that attracted you to that man? Was your trip just to see a reed shaken in the wind?"

Of course not. If they wanted to see and listen to weak, vacillating people, they could have found them in the temple. Such people were all over the place, like the common reeds to which Jesus referred.

John was neither common nor compromising, and he didn't hold back his message from anybody. In Matthew 3, when all of the religious leaders visited him, he had his big moment of opportunity to play to the crowd. But in verses 7–10, rather than coddle them, he delivered the short, sharp shock of biblical truth: "Brood of vipers! Who warned you to flee from the wrath to come? Therefore bear fruits worthy of repentance, and do not think to say to yourselves, 'We have Abraham as our father.' For I say to you that God is able to raise up children to Abraham from these stones. And even now the ax is laid to the root of the trees."

Then he went on to talk about a judgment of purging and burning and unquenchable fire—a devastating diatribe against those religious leaders. The whole leadership of Israel had let Herod's sin of adultery and his illicit marriage go unchallenged. But John faced him, nose to nose, and told him it was a sin. That's why Herod imprisoned John, who was soon to have his head chopped off and brought into a party on a plate. John was a man who well understood the idea that the great colonial defender of religious liberty, William Penn, expressed centuries later: "Right is right even if everyone is against it, and wrong is wrong even if everyone is for it."

## STRENGTH IN SELF-DENIAL

Another element of greatness John revealed was self-denial. Truly great people are those who can deny themselves. When I look back in history at great generals who risked their troops and their own lives for victory, or at scientists who shut themselves up in their laboratories for months or even years, trying to discover something we now take for granted, or at a missionary who burned his life out by the time he was thirty, trying to get the gospel to some people in a foreign land, I remind myself that this is the mark of greatness. If the desire for comfort is always diverting you, if you can't take pain and you've always got to find the easy way, then you'll never know what greatness is.

John the Baptist lived in the wilderness. His cause was not comfort, though I'm sure there were many times when he wished he had it. He wasn't trying to see if he could just hang around long enough to fall into the gravy, like so many people who wait passively, hoping something will happen to make life easy for them. He was not interested in gaining favor from leaders, religious or otherwise. He stood apart, unstained by the system.

John's commitment was all-consuming. According to Luke 1:15, an angel predicted he would "drink neither wine nor strong drink." Indeed, John took a Nazarite vow, which removed him from the guest lists for all the fancy banquets and social events where drinking took place. It also was part of the Nazarite vow not to cut your hair, which didn't exactly keep you up with contemporary fashion trends.

Through his lifestyle, John was saying, "I don't care about what I look like. I don't care about indulging myself in the delicacies of life. I am given to a cause." Many people took a Nazarite vow for a few weeks or a few months, but less than a handful took it for life: Samson, Samuel, John the Baptist.

## POINTLESS PENANCE

Let's make an important distinction between self-denial and penance. Self-denial is giving up creature comforts to work toward a worthy goal. Penance is self-punishment in hopes of earning God's favor, which is absolutely, 100 percent impossible—and 100 percent unnecessary. No one can be good enough, or make himself feel bad enough, to earn his way into heaven. But no one has to, because Jesus paid the full price of entry on behalf of all true Christians.

Even so, history gives many, many gruesome examples of tragically misguided penitents. Saint Assepsumas thought he could rid himself of sin through self-inflicted pain, and he wore so many chains that he had to crawl around on his hands and knees. Makarios the Younger sat naked in a swamp for six months, until mosquito bites made him look like a victim of leprosy. Saint Marin spent eleven years in a hollowed-out tree. Great contribution to society.

Agnes de Roucher was the only daughter of one of the wealthiest merchants in Paris, and all the neighborhood admired her beauty and virtue. Her father died, leaving her his entire estate. She determined to become a recluse and spend the remainder of her days in a narrow cell built within the wall of a church. The bishop of Paris, attended by his chaplains and the canons of Notre Dame, entered the cell and celebrated a pontifical mass. Then, after the poor thing had bidden adieu to her friends and relations, Agnes ordered the masons to fill up the opening except for a small hole so she could watch and hear the offices of the church. She was eighteen when she went in and died at age eighty, never having come out. In all that time, no one ever told her Jesus was the key to redemption. God help such mistaken piety.

## THE RIGHT MAN FOR THE JOB

Another indicator of the greatness of John the Baptist was his privileged calling: to announce the arrival of God in human flesh. The only person in the human race who even comes close to John in that regard is Mary, whom God chose to bear the Messiah. But in many ways, John was greater than Mary. Mary gave birth to a baby; John heralded a king. Mary brought Jesus into thirty years of obscurity; John ushered Him into three years of monumental ministry.

In fact, this man was so remarkable that Luke 3:15 says people thought he was the Messiah: "Now as the people were in expectation, and all reasoned in their hearts about John, whether he was the Christ or not." I can scarcely imagine what it would have been like to hear John speak, but he was dynamic, articulate, confrontational, powerful—the greatest prophet God had ever called.

True greatness always matches the right man with the right position. A man could have potential greatness, but if he never got into the right field, he'd never know that. Many people in the world just sort of grab a job, and if they're "lucky" enough, their talent will intersect with their calling. But as Christians, we have God to give us that direction.

And so the man and the mission came together. Amos 3:7 says: "Surely the LORD God does nothing, / Unless He reveals His secret to His servants the prophets." John was a man who had a message from God. It had been four hundred years since a prophet had come, and when John was born, God broke His silence. John spoke with power and conviction and influenced people with his inspired words. Many believed his message, and everybody knew he was a prophet.

He not only predicted the Messiah, he baptized the Messiah. So he was not just one who tells, he was one who does. He touched the living Christ and was the forerunner of Christ, the baptizer of Christ, the prophet who was also the fulfillment of prophecy.

## MAKING WAVES

A great man has to be in the right place at the right time. After four centuries without a prophet, the Jews felt electricity in the air when John came on the scene. Another element of John's greatness, then, was that he became the focal point; he became pivotal at that juncture of redemptive history; the action took place all around him. He was the culmination of all of Old Testament history.

He made waves. He upset the status quo. He had high impact. He created conflict. He stirred up a hornet's nest. When he confronted the Jews, situations became explosive. He brought everything to a head. Everywhere he moved, he caused a violent reaction. He was a man of destiny, the eye of the hurricane. There's something exciting about that sort of man. Great figures in world events have a way of leaving a cloud of dust. A flurry of activity always surrounds them because they move through history generating such passion and change.

In Matthew 11:12, Jesus observed that John's preaching led to violence: "And from the days of John the Baptist until now the kingdom of heaven suffers violence, and the violent take it by force." In other words, "Ever since he's been around, we've had problems." John's life had become the issue, his ministry had become the focus.

There are two possible ways to translate this verse based on the way you read a verb in the middle, *biazo*. It can be translated as passive, meaning something else is acting upon it, or reflexive, meaning it is acting on itself. Translated passively, verse 12 would read this way: "The kingdom of heaven is suffering violence and violent men are seizing it." That's the way one translation (KJV) has it: "The kingdom of heaven suffereth violence, and the violent take it by force."

In other words, "Here comes God, God's messenger, and God's Messiah, representing God's rule and His kingdom, which is suffering violence. It is being persecuted." In fact, persecution had broken out against John the Baptist; he was already in prison. The Pharisees and the scribes had vigorously attacked the kingdom. They had vigorously rejected Jesus Christ.

The Jews were adamantly rejecting the kingdom. They were not accepting the kingdom in its spiritual dimension by receiving the Messiah, so they couldn't accept the kingdom in its earthly dimension and receive the millennial kingdom either. Soon they would not only kill the preacher, but the King Himself. In the midst of all this, John's message was so decisive that it created a violent reaction. Violent men were trying to stop the advance of the kingdom.

But let's assume we translate it reflexively, which is equally correct. Then it would read: "The kingdom of heaven is vigorously pressing itself forward and forceful people are eagerly taking it." This means the very opposite of the other translation: the kingdom is moving ahead, and forceful people are entering it. This says that John the Baptist was effective: he was moving ahead, and the kingdom was pressing vigorously or violently forward as he careened, without apology, through the sinfulness of the world.

History tells us that's exactly what happened. John the Baptist had an amazing, dramatic impact. People were turning to God, they were repenting of their sins, and he was leading many to Christ, as the angel Gabriel foretold in Luke 1:16: "And He will turn many of the children of Israel to the Lord their God."

If we take the reflexive interpretation, then, the kingdom was moving ahead vigorously. Our Lord was continuing to mark out the greatness of John. Through him the kingdom was on the move. He was God's tool to purify the people and get them ready. That is the meaning of a parallel statement in Luke 16:16, which says: "The law and the prophets were until John. Since that time the kingdom of God has been preached, and everyone is pressing into it." That passage makes it safer to say that this is a reflexive use of *biazo*, that the kingdom was moving ahead under the power of this marvelous man, John, and vigorous, aggressive, forceful people were taking that kingdom.

Does that express the proper perspective on salvation? *Yes!* Entrance into the kingdom requires earnest endeavor, untiring energy, and utmost exertion, because Satan is mighty, his demons are powerful, and sin holds us fast. God can break that hold and free our hearts to respond. The kingdom is not for weaklings and compromisers; it is not for the half-committed, the lovers of the world, or the shallow disciples who want to hold on to the stuff that perishes. The kingdom is for those who are willing to affirm their desperate need for salvation from sin and seize the offer of grace.

## TRUE GREATNESS

John was the final culmination of the message that began in Genesis with the promise of "the seed of the woman" who would crush Satan's head. This promise filled the Scriptures until the moment he pointed to the living Christ: "The Messiah is coming! The Messiah is coming!" The kingdom was moving violently through the godless, human system. And eager, vigorous people were pressing into it. This was the climax; everything had built up to John.

In Matthew 11:14, Jesus stated, "And if you are willing to receive it, he is Elijah who is to come." In the Old Testament, Malachi 4:5 said that before the Messiah came to set up His kingdom on earth,

Elijah would come as a forerunner. In Matthew, Jesus wasn't saying John was actually Elijah, but one like Elijah. John 1 bears this out, when the priests and Levites asked John if he were the Christ, and he said he wasn't. Then in John 1:21, they asked, "'What then? Are you Elijah?' He said, 'I am not.'" We know Jesus' meaning in Matthew is that someone in the person and character of Elijah had come: a powerful, rugged, Elijah-like individual who was announcing the kingdom.

So, according to Jesus, John the Baptist was the greatest mortal who ever lived, yet amazingly Matthew 11:11 says, "He who is least in the kingdom of heaven is greater than he." This is a great truth. Greatness isn't being like John the Baptist, because his was a greatness of function as herald for Christ. True greatness is not in our function, but in our relationship to God that places us in His kingdom.

But the religious intellectuals didn't believe and didn't enter the kingdom. Even with John's powerful culmination of Old Testament history, his privileged calling, and his personal character, not everybody believed, and not everybody understood the significance of this man. They were attracted to him, but not to the Savior and His salvation message. So the Lord added a warning in Matthew 11:15: "He who has ears to hear, let him hear!"

This was a way of saying, "If John is the forerunner, then I am the King. And if I am the King, I am offering the kingdom. And that puts all of you in the place of making a choice. Don't refuse it. If you receive Me as the Messiah, I'll bring the millennial kingdom to earth." A few received the King, and His kingdom came into their hearts. An earthly kingdom yet awaits, when He returns and all receive Him.

## A DIFFERENT KIND OF MESSENGER

Many people rejected John the Baptist because they wanted a different kind of messenger. Yet when they heard from the ultimate

Messenger, Jesus Christ, these same people complained about Him even more harshly. Nothing He said convinced them to confess sin and repent. The longer He preached, the angrier they became. There was no validity in their criticism; they just hated His indictment.

And the same thing happens today. People don't want to hear the truth, no matter what it is, because they're not seeking truth. They're not open to truth. They won't acknowledge their sin, and they aren't interested in a Savior, so they just sit back and criticize or get angry.

Years ago, at the height of the women's lib movement, I did a series of sermons on God's role for women and what God desires for them. I just preached on the fact that women are to love their husbands, love their children, and be keepers at home. This biblical truth made the women's liberation leaders furious. They marched on our church; all the networks covered it, and a picture of the protest appeared on the front page of the *Los Angeles Times*. (I expect the fact that our attendance went up a thousand in a week, as a result of their efforts, further enraged the protesters!)

Some people refuse to accept gospel truth before they even hear it. When Phil Donahue was at the height of his popularity, his producers repeatedly invited me to go on his show. It was called a "talk" show, but rather than talking, the guests spent a lot of time arguing, fending off verbal attacks, and being baited by Phil or another guest. It was the predecessor of many more such shows since. I wouldn't do it. The person who called said, "I don't think you know who's calling. This is *Phil Donahue*." I would not go because of the show's atmosphere of assault and attack. The normal approach seemed to demean people whose views they rejected, interrupting them before they could complete a thought. I felt they wouldn't be interested in what I had to say about the gospel, that they just wanted to use me to discredit biblical truth. That's no way to find truth. The gospel is to be proclaimed, not debated.

In Matthew 11:16, Jesus began a pointed response to the insufferable grumps before Him with a standard phrase that was very familiar, "But to what shall I liken this generation?" In the Midrash, a compilation of Jewish traditional teaching, that's the most common formula for introducing a parable. All good teachers know that they have to teach in word pictures or analogies, in similes, metaphors, or figures of speech to make their points clearly. That was true with the rabbis, who traditionally began their parables with this question, meaning, "How can I illustrate what this generation is like?"

Jesus continued, "It is like children sitting in the marketplaces and calling to their companions, and saying: / 'We played the flute for you, / And you did not dance; / We mourned to you, / And you did not lament'" (vv. 16–17).

In the center of every town was a town square or modest public park called the *agora* in Greek, which means marketplace. On market days, the people filled up that open space with all of their carts and stalls and merchandise. Naturally it was a favorite place for the children to run around, and it never took them long to find their friends and start playing games together.

As they do today, children often played games that mimicked the lives of their families. One of the popular games was "Wedding" and another favorite—though a little harder for us to imagine—was "Funeral." These were the major public social events the children saw all the time. Whenever a wedding occurred, a great processional always strode through town that included the bride, the bridegroom, friends of the groom, all of the ladies who were waiting on the bride, and everybody else in the wedding. Along behind them came neighbors and townspeople playing pipes and flutes, skipping and hopping and dancing with joy.

Very likely, while their parents were busy buying, selling, and gossiping at the market, these kids got together to playact a wedding of their own. Some fortunate girl was the bride, a boy was the groom, and the other children took on the various roles. They got the whole procession going through the *agora*, and somebody who could blow a whistle or play a little flute did so. As they passed other friends of theirs, they called out, "Come on, join the procession!"

After they did that a while, they played "Funeral." A funeral procession was just as inevitable and as public as a wedding. Mourners lifted up the body and carried it through the city, followed by all the family. The family hired women who were professional wailers to come along, moaning and lamenting. It was also very common in funeral processions for people to beat on their chests and heads or all over their bodies. The kids played this by walking in a procession, yelling and pretending to beat on themselves. And once again, they shouted to their other friends to come play with them.

But some kids didn't want to play. The kids in this parable were just spoilsports you can almost hear saying, "We don't want to play your dumb game!"

So the group said, "Okay, we'll change our game. If you don't like 'Wedding,' we'll play 'Funeral'"—the opposite extreme. But the answer came back, "We don't want to play that either. We don't want to be involved at all. Just leave us alone." That's the idea in Matthew 11:17: "Hey, we played the flute and you didn't respond, so we mourned, and you didn't react to that either."

Peevish children. The sad game is the total opposite of the glad game, but no matter how their friends worked to accommodate them, they weren't going to play. They preferred to sit stubbornly on the sidelines and criticize—a prime example of the sheer obstinacy and perversity of human nature.

## NO SATISFACTION

The principle of the parable is perfectly clear. Some people just don't want to play, no matter what the game is, and no matter how you approach them. They'll criticize the wedding and they'll criticize the funeral. Nothing satisfies them. They will always find fault because, at heart, they are unwilling to participate, unwilling to be satisfied.

Jesus said that generation behaved like those children. "You're like the children who, when called by their little friends, had no openness and no interest, but just a bitter, critical, contrary spirit."

The application comes in Matthew 11:18–19: "For John came neither eating nor drinking, and they say, 'He has a demon.' The Son of Man came eating and drinking, and they say, 'Look, a glutton and a winebibber, a friend of tax collectors and sinners!' But wisdom is justified by her children."

John, we might say, came in funeral mode. He was austere, dressed in camel's hair (which was black), ate locusts and wild honey, lived in the desert as a hermit, and had no normal social relationships. He came pounding the message of judgment and fiery condemnation. He talked about an ax chopping at the root of the tree. He called for repentance and the demonstration of the fruit of repentance. He was a voice crying in the wilderness.

This weird behavior convinced people that John was demon possessed. Anybody who acted like that had to be off his rocker and worse. Yet Scripture tells us these same people rejoiced in his presence for a season. He was without equal. He had the power of personality to attract them. And they basked in his light for a little while. But the critics among them finally just said, "Ah, he's nuts!" They equated madness with demon possession.

They made that connection, I think, because it commonly was true. There was the maniac of Gadara, who was possessed with a legion of demons. He was also deranged, cutting himself up, running around naked, living in caves and tombs (Luke 8:26–36). So they simply reasoned that anybody who was as strange as John, to live the way he lived, must be possessed of a demon. Instead of seeing his lifestyle as a rebuke to their indulgence, they just ridiculed him.

On the other hand, following John came the Son of Man. And Jesus used His human title in Matthew 11:19 to underscore His coming in His humanness, eating and drinking. Jesus was in the opposite of John's funeral style. He was in wedding mode. He got into the flow of social life. He had meals with people, stayed in their homes, and attended local activities. You could find Him at social events, including weddings. He made wine. He went to the synagogue. He was in the temple. He walked from village to village. He was by the sea with the fishermen and sailed with them. He was wherever they were, a part of their lives, sharing food and drink with them.

As a matter of fact, in Matthew 9:14–15, the disciples of John, who were used to the funeral mode, went to the disciples of Jesus and said, "Hey, why don't you fast like we fast?" And the answer was, in effect, "Well, you don't fast at a wedding!" In other words, "The Messiah is here, and this is a celebration."

## CRITICS' CHOICE

The Lord came in a very different way from John, and they still resented Him, calling Him a gluttonous winebibber who socialized with tax collectors and sinners. Because He mingled, they criticized. But because John didn't mingle, they criticized him. The phrase here for a gluttonous man, *anthromopos phagos*, has no dignity whatever. It's a nondescript term indicating someone who ate to excess, someone who just sat around and stuffed food in his mouth. Then they claimed Jesus was also a winebibber, someone who drank too much, too often. What the Lord did drink was concentrated wine mixed with water, which would stimulate about as much as our tea or coffee.

Jesus wove Himself into the tapestry of daily life. He got involved, unlike John the Baptist, who lived in the wilderness and didn't cultivate fine manners or the gift of hospitality. And for His efforts, Jesus was labeled with the riffraff. Because Jesus came mixing with hurting, needy people, sharing their sorrows and their joys, His critics said He was a rounder. On the other hand, because John came living in the desert, fasting, despising food, and isolated from people, they said he was mad and demonic. The whole point is that they were just critical, period. Nothing anyone could do would please them.

William Barclay wisely said,

> The plain fact is that when people do not want to listen to the truth, they will easily enough find an excuse for not listening. They do not even try to be consistent in their criticism. They'll criticize the same person and the same institution from quite opposite grounds and reasons. If people are determined to make no response, they will remain stubbornly and sullenly unresponsive no matter what invitation is made to them.[1]

Our Lord pointed out that no matter what He did, the Jewish establishment just wouldn't play. Their peevish, contrary, critical hearts held them captive. It was the wrong response, as Matthew 11:19 underscores: "But wisdom is justified by her children." This means the fruit of wisdom is visible to everyone, and so are the consequences of refusing God's truth. Jesus was saying, in effect, "You sit back and criticize, no matter what John or I do; no matter what our message is, you attack. But in the end, the truth will justify itself by what it produces. You can criticize Christ, but you're going to run into trouble when you look at the people whose lives He has changed. You can criticize the church, but then you have to explain why the church has had the impact it has had on the world."

Truth or wisdom ultimately is justified by what it produces. That is an unanswerable argument. The wisdom of John the Baptist that insisted on repentance, and the wisdom of Jesus that insisted on repentance, were shown to be justified by what they accomplished in the hearts and the lives of people who believed.

Some people are just die-hard critics. You can't avoid them, and you can't win them over, whether you try to spin the gospel to suit their tastes or you tell the truth and hope God will work in their hearts. They're not even looking for the truth. They just want to find everything wrong with Christ and Christianity, which is a tragic response. In the end, the truth will be justified by what it produces. And they may not know the truth until it's too late.

# 10

## TRAITORS TO THE FAITH

The gospel is hard to believe and requires denial of oneself. Yet the rewards of believing and making that sacrifice are beyond measure. Yes, the gate is narrow, and the truth is hard. But the trade-off is eternal life with God in heaven! Why should we have to soft-pedal a message that's so incredibly wonderful? Why would anybody stonewall information, however distasteful or inconvenient it is on the surface, that will send him to heaven *forever*? And why, once he heard and apparently believed the gospel, would he ever turn away from it?

Not long ago, a friend of mine shared the heartbreaking story of a son who grew up in a church, hearing of the Word of God, who nevertheless turned his back on Christ and entered fully into the homosexual community in San Francisco. I know of far too many tragic cases where men have turned their backs on their wives, their families, and their Lord and walked away. These people didn't start out as skeptics outside the church, but as people whom the Word of Christ had nurtured. Yet they ultimately rejected the truth of the gospel.

You've probably had a similar experience with someone you know. I've already recounted the stories of three of my closest friends—one in high school, one in college, and one in seminary—who seemed so dedicated to serving the Lord, and yet all of them eventually turned their backs on Him. One became a dope-smoking rock-concert promoter, and another became a Buddhist. These were not casual acquaintances, but friends at a very close level. I was sure they shared my passion for the true gospel as much as they shared my love for sports.

These three young men proved to me that you can profess Christ and not know Him. You can think you're a Christian and later see clearly that you're not; you can certainly deceive other people. Seeing these seemingly intelligent, dedicated, strong Christians abandon their beliefs forced me to think about who is really a Christian and what being a Christian really means. Their actions portrayed them as fellow soldiers of Christ, but in the end their hearts exposed them as traitors.

Spiritual defectors are an integral part of the story of Christianity, both past and present. They're in your life and mine, just as they were in Jesus' life. They shouldn't surprise you, defeat you, disappoint you, or cause you to despair. Jesus' insights on spiritual defectors in John 6, and the reaction to His teaching about the issue, give us one of the most compelling and enlightening stories of His ministry. It's worth considering closely.

## SPIRITUAL DEFECTORS

A defector is a traitor. I expect you've had the wrenching experience of seeing someone you have loved and worked with in the Lord defect from the gospel. Nothing is more painful to me than that. But we can take some comfort in knowing that Jesus endured far more heartbreaking defections and can offer sympathy to us in our suffering such disappointments.

It's a pattern appearing time and again throughout Scripture. In Philippians 2:20, Paul wrote, "For I have no one like-minded, who will sincerely care for your state." In 2 Timothy 1:15, he said, "This you know, that all those in Asia have turned away from me, among whom are Phygellus and Hermogenes."

Defections are not limited only to those of us on this side of the cross. Exodus 32:7: "And the LORD said to Moses"—who was on Mount Sinai—"Go, get down! For your people whom you brought out of the land of Egypt have corrupted themselves." While Moses was receiving the Law, they were making a golden calf to worship.

Isaiah 22:12 pictures God calling His people to join in his sorrow over defecting, deserting Israel: "And in that day the Lord GOD of hosts / Called for weeping and for mourning." Jesus wept for them, too, says Luke 19:41: "Now as He drew near, He saw the city and wept over it." Those who claim to belong to God yet defect have broken God's heart.

When you catalog your influence on others, you may be discouraged at the number of people you've attended church or Bible study with who have become traitors to the faith. I've had that experience repeatedly through my life and ministry, sometimes with people I've taught and known personally for decades. I find a measure of comfort in the apostle Paul's experience, because I can't imagine anyone walking with him, seeing his life, ministering alongside him, being touched by the profound character of the man and by his immense mind, and then turning away from Jesus Christ, as his friend Demas did (2 Tim. 4:10).

What turns the hearers of the true gospel away? Why is it that some people, who are attracted to Jesus and the Word of God, are only temporary followers? What are the characteristics of a spiritual defector? What, in the end, *can* we do and *should* we do to witness to them? What did Jesus do, and what can we learn from His example?

John 6, as we shall see in a minute, gives us a remarkably complete list of implied characteristics of spiritual defectors, reasons why people who seem to embrace the gospel ultimately turn away from it. Understanding them will help you see how futile it is to invent a user-friendly gospel to appeal to one target audience or another. It will also help you prepare for the rejection the truth is likely to receive. *No matter how many features or enticements you add, and how many difficulties you remove, all except true believers will turn you down in the end.* But as Jesus' example so compellingly shows, that very rejection is proof of the power of the gospel. To the degree it is watered down, it ceases to be a threat to a sinful and self-absorbed world; to the degree it remains powerful, the unrepentant and proud will flee from it in fear. And rightly so.

This is one of the most serious problems with seeker-sensitive churches. I was talking to a pastor at a seeker-friendly church not long ago about his idea that prospective Christians needed to "feel welcome" and "accepted" before anything else: no "threats," no "judgmental baggage."

I asked, "If you had a person living in sin come to your church, would you confront him?"

He furrowed his brow and shook his head disapprovingly. "Oh, no! We'd want him to feel loved and welcome."

My eyes widened. "How long would it be before you would actually say something about that?"

"Maybe a year and a half, two years," he said, smiling. "Because then he would really feel a part of things."

That was shocking to me. Is there some virtue in leaving a man in his sin for the sake of feeling accepted? "Well, that's the difference between your church and our church," I said finally. "Openly practicing sinners come to our church, and they either get saved or they don't come back."

## THE ROAR OF THE CROWD

People defect from the gospel because they were drawn to it initially for the wrong reasons. The excitement of the crowd, not the meaning of the message, lures them at first. A lively crowd, and the production value of a worship service emphasizing showmanship rather than Scripture, wows the modern-day seeker.

John 6 begins with the incredible miracle of Jesus feeding the five thousand on a few small loaves and fishes. This is the only miracle of Jesus that appears in all four gospels, a decisive demonstration of the deity of Christ. What a contrast this chapter brings, beginning with the best-documented miracle of Jesus' earthly ministry, and ending with perhaps half of His followers abandoning Him.

John 6:1–2 begins, "After these things Jesus went over the Sea of Galilee, which is the Sea of Tiberias. Then a great multitude followed Him, because they saw His signs which He performed on those who were diseased." The miracles initially attracted both true and false disciples. Jesus had been ministering in Galilee for many months. By now His healings and deliverance from demons and even death had brought Him immense popularity. Jesus had banished disease from Galilee. The crowds had grown larger and larger, and Jesus had become the most popular person in the history of Galilee, then or ever since. Jesus was the event of a lifetime, and His popularity had drawn massive mobs. His TV ratings would have been through the roof.

Popularity didn't help. When Jesus was popular, He attracted the most shallow fun-seekers. Genuine disciples were drawn not by showbiz but by the truth, the power, and the character of His message.

Christianity has to be very careful when it is popular. The action and excitement of a crowd captivate people. They gather in a sports stadium, or a large auditorium or church, to be part of a big event. There's an energy, almost a pep-rally feel, but many of the participants are there for the crowd, not the Crown. They're looking for some miraculous intervention on their behalf, or the promise of something they can cash in on. Or just a good show.

## SUPERNATURAL ATTRACTION

Another reason for defections from the gospel is that defectors are overly distracted by the supernatural. Miracles and power displays are fertile ground for superficial disciples. A great crowd followed Jesus and it was time for them all to eat, but the only food anybody could find was a meager meal one boy in the audience was carrying. John 6:8–9 tells us: "One of His disciples, Andrew, Simon Peter's brother, said to Him, 'There is a lad here who has five barley loaves'"—these would have been like little flat crackers—"and two small fish"—probably pickled fish. They used to spread the pickled fish on the cracker, or just lay it on top—"but what are they among so many?" Andrew was saying, "This situation is hopeless. We've scoured the crowd, and all we've found is one kid with a few crackers and some pickled fish."

Verse 10 says: "Then Jesus said, 'Make the people sit down'"— which is another way of saying, "Get them all ready for dinner." "Now there was much grass in the place. So the men sat down, in number about five thousand." That number would easily double with the women and children and could well have been twenty thousand or more.

Verse 11 reveals what He served them: "And Jesus took the loaves, and when He had given thanks He distributed them to the disciples, and the disciples to those sitting down; and likewise of the fish, as much as they wanted." Where was the showmanship? Jesus had performed an awesome miracle in the most understated way possible. Shouldn't the account say, "And heaven *thundered* and the earth *shook* and fish started *flying* out of the Sea of Galilee and diving into little baskets, and biscuits started *sailing* out of the sky, and the angels *sang*"? There's no spotlight whatsoever.

Then we learn, in verse 13, that there were twelve baskets of food left over, probably more than all the disciples could eat at the next meal. The Greek word for basket, *kophinos*, is the source of the English word "coffin" and means a large, heavy basket. There was plenty to spare.

Here was the real attraction for the crowd: Just show up, and Jesus gives you all the food you can eat. Wow! Suddenly, from spending most of their days earning enough to feed themselves and preparing meals, they were looking at a life of leisure. A welfare state! His miracles had always fascinated them, but this one was beyond anything else. Sure, you need healing once in a while, but you need dinner every day.

Christianity has always attracted thrill-seekers fascinated by Jesus' image as a wonder-worker and life transformer who changes people and blesses His own. A preoccupation with miracles is one of the immense dangers in the charismatic movement today, because it attracts people on the premise that miracles are waiting for you to grab for yourself. There are televangelists ready to hand over miracles to you right now, if you'll just call this toll-free number and make your pledge. They want to claim the power of miracles the way Simon did in Acts 8:9; he "practiced sorcery in the city and astonished the people of Samaria, claiming that he was someone great."

To some false followers of Christ, the real appeal is the crowd. It could be their family, their ancestors, their friends, the group they run in, their Christian associates, or the "in" crowd to which they aspire. But if the attraction itself is nothing more than a supernatural stage extravaganza, the appeal will be shallow and temporary. As soon as they get a glimpse of what the gospel is really all about and the sacrifice required, they're history.

## THE HERE AND NOW

Another characteristic of defectors is that they think only of earthly things. John 6:14 continues, "Then those men, when they had seen the sign that Jesus did, said, 'This is truly the Prophet who is to come into the world.'" They meant the Messiah prophesied and promised in Deuteronomy 18:15. The King is here!

And they knew just what to do in the next verse: "Therefore when Jesus perceived that they were about to come and take Him by force to make Him king, He departed again to the mountain by Himself alone." They had an earthly kingdom in mind. If He could create enough loaves and fish to feed twenty thousand people, certainly He could dish out what the Romans deserved, give them the boot, and liberate Israel.

But if they believed spiritually that He was the great Messiah, where was the adoration? Where were the worship and respect? They never got past thinking of Jesus as an earthly king who would give them the earthly freedom and revenge they wanted. They had no interest in "Thy kingdom come, Thy will be done." Rather they were saying, "*Our* kingdom come, *our* will be fulfilled."

All they wanted to do was force Him to be their personal miracle-worker and use His power politically and militarily against the Romans. Instead of falling on their faces to worship the Promised One as their Savior from sin and judgment, they wanted to push Him into following their own earthly agenda. This is typical of defectors. They look at Jesus as the one who's going to solve their daily dilemmas, fix their lives, meet their needs and desires, and make them rich.

Try to sell the gospel on that basis, and people will come to you for all the wrong reasons. You cannot call people to Christ because it's the thing to do and everybody's doing it. You can't call people to Christ to get swell miracles or have their lives straightened out. This is the lie of the health-wealth-prosperity gospel and the felt-needs gospel, and all it does is draw people in who soon become disillusioned. As Jesus said in John 18:36, "My kingdom is not of this world."

A person who had once professed Christ wrote me a letter, saying, "Your Jesus didn't work. My husband left, my son's in the hospital and I have a terminal illness. Your Jesus didn't work!" The shallow follower has no sense of the spiritual, the eternal and divine, no particular love for God or attachment to Jesus Christ. The shallow Christian lives for the here and now; and if Jesus doesn't deliver, that's the end of it.

## NO LONGING FOR WORSHIP

False Christians have no desire for true worship. Back in John 4:23, Jesus defined salvation as worship when He said, "The Father is seeking such to worship Him." People ask me how to determine whether people are Christians or not. You can't necessarily tell by watching them, because some non-Christians live outwardly moral lives, while some Christians sin in visible, public ways. You can't tell by listening to them; if you listen long enough, the truth will probably come out, but some people guard their tongues very well. The way you can tell a person is truly a Christian is by what he desires. If he longs to praise and worship God and Christ, that is evidence of a transformed heart.

In the next few verses of John 6, the disciples sailed on the Sea of Galilee toward Capernaum, leaving Jesus behind as He told them to do. The true test of their discipleship is made manifest in verse 18: "Then the sea arose because a great wind was blowing." Anybody who has ever been on the Sea of Galilee can certainly understand this. The Sea of Galilee is below sea level and surrounded by mountains. Dry desert winds called siroccos come racing down the canyons and swirl out onto the lake with so much force that they make big, rough whitecaps.

The next verse continues the story: "So when they had rowed about three or four miles, they saw Jesus walking on the sea and drawing near the boat; and they were afraid." Here again, if Jesus thought a good show would save people, He missed His chance. No heavenly trumpets or bolts of lightning announced His presence. It was just so matter-of-fact. Yet the setting here is a storm at sea in the middle of the night. A boatload of men were exhausted after hours of battling the rough water, and they had no idea whether they were going to live or die. Then all of a sudden, they looked out, and there was Jesus, walking on the sea toward the boat.

John tells us they were frightened. I'd panic too. Nobody walks on water. The parallel passage in Matthew adds that Peter climbed out of the boat and started walking on the water himself toward Jesus, but "when he saw that the wind was boisterous, he was afraid; and beginning to sink he cried out saying, 'Lord, save me!'" (14:30). In his excitement and impetuousness, Peter jumped out of the little boat, but then he took a look at his surroundings and said to himself, "What in the world am I doing out here?"

No doubt the disciples were afraid of the storm, but they were far more afraid of the One walking on the water, who was none other than God Himself. The next verse is key: "But He said to them, 'It is I; do not be afraid'" (John 6:20). He stilled the storm, and immediately the boat was at its destination. The storm was quieted, and instantaneously they went from wherever they were to the shore. The text almost sounds as if they traveled there miraculously, without crossing the water. And Matthew says, "They worshipped Him" (see 14:33).

Some believers never fall down in adoring wonder. Their perspective is strictly utilitarian: "What are You going to do for me, Jesus? I want to follow You because this is where the action is. And I could use a few more miracles myself." There is no eager prostration in worship before the Lord.

But the true disciples are there, too, and their actions separate them from the rest. As Matthew 14:33 puts it, "Then those who were in the boat came and worshiped Him." Look at people who claim to be Christians, and see how deeply they worship the Lord. See how they sing the songs. Ask them what their prayer lives are like. How important is it for them to be in church on the Lord's Day? Is Jesus Christ the love of their lives? Is it obvious?

You can tell, if you look closely enough. True believers show a deep humility, a sense of genuine respect for and awe of Jesus Christ. Are they marked by adoring wonder? If they aren't, they won't stay with those who are, no matter how appealing you try to make it. If they are, you can't keep them away, no matter how stark or challenging the truth.

## LOOKING FOR A HANDOUT

A defector from the faith seeks personal gain, not an opportunity to worship. We see this in the action of the crowd after it realizes Jesus has left and traveled to Capernaum. Did those people all return to where He fed them and preached the day before because they wanted to worship? No, they wanted free breakfast!

In a time when getting enough to eat was a difficult, endless job, free food was an instant ticket to ease. The crowd went to Capernaum for the wrong reason; John 6:25: "And when they found Him on the other side of the sea, they said to Him, 'Rabbi, when did you come here?'" They came to the other side of the lake probably expecting breakfast. All they could think of was personal fulfillment through His miracles: meet *my* needs, supply what *I* want, feed *me*.

Then the next verse: "Jesus answered them and said, 'Most assuredly, I say to you, you seek Me, not because you saw the signs, but because you ate of the loaves and were filled." It's an indictment: "You're here for one thing, and that's because you're hungry." The Greek word for "filled" is used of animals and means to be "foddered up." These people were real candidates for the prosperity gospel.

"Make me wealthy, make me prosperous, make me successful, fulfill all my desires, and do it now . . . I demand it!"

Jesus continued, "Do not labor for the food which perishes, but for the food which endures to everlasting life, which the Son of Man will give you, because God the Father has set His seal on Him" (John 6:27). He was saying, "You're looking for the wrong stuff! You're talking about breakfast, and I'm talking about eternal life."

How many people do the same thing every day: come into the church and turn their backs on eternal life? That's why we have to preach on hell. That's why we have to warn people about what is to come in the next life. People need to understand what they're doing. It's fine to be drawn in by the crowd and fascinated by the supernatural power of Jesus. But at some point, you must worship and come to grips with eternal matters.

This point deeply concerns me about most of the popular evangelical fads today. What kind of people are they attracting? Lured by the crowd and the promise of something supernatural, thinking only of earthly things with little desire for true worship, but plenty of desire for personal prosperity, they do not understand eternal issues. Until they do and confess their need, *they will never be saved.*

## THE QUEST FOR POWER

Spiritual defectors make demands on God. They come barreling into church with the attitude (whether spoken or not): "Okay, God, I'm going to give You six months to deliver, and if You don't, I'm outta here!"

John 6:28: "Then they said to Him, 'What shall we do, that we may work the works of God?'" What they were really saying was, "All right, our first demand is: Give us the power! Are You saying You're not going to make our breakfast? Then give us the power to do it ourselves, so we can work the works of God."

This is identical to Acts 8:18–19. Simon saw the power of God displayed through Peter and he offered to buy it, more or less, saying, "I want that power. How much?" Many people in Christian churches are trying somehow to get the power—and speakers are encouraging them! They say, "Folks, we want *you* to get the *power*." Then, wild, crazy things go on with people jumping and hollering and screaming and flipping and flopping all over the place for one basic thing: they're trying to get the power.

I think about this when I watch those frantic, overdressed evangelists on television, raving and promising people power. Then people in the crowd, in a mindless acquiescence to an altered state of consciousness—wanting so desperately to get the power that they'll do anything the speaker suggests—fall over in a faint. It's a sad situation when people want the power more than they want the Person. No one on earth can have the power of Jesus Christ to do what He did, and anybody who promises otherwise is lying.

God granted the power of Jesus Christ only to the apostles and those who followed in the apostolic age to establish His messiahship. You will never have the power to heal the sick or raise the dead, walk on water, or cast out demons. But anyone can be saved who believes in Him.

The Lord's response to the people's question came in John 6:29: "Jesus answered and said to them, 'This is the work of God, that you believe in Him whom He sent.'" But they were not interested in that believing stuff, so in verse 30 they made another demand: "Therefore they said to Him, 'What sign will You perform then, that we may see it and believe You? What work will You do?'" In other words, "Do some more miracles and tricks to prove You're worth our faith."

What they were really thinking about was how they were going to put Him in a corner. "We believe in You, Jesus, if You make breakfast." They had just seen a monumental miracle, and they wanted more. Thrill-seekers never have enough signs and wonders. That's the sad thing about trying to draw people into Christianity with the promise of a miracle. The promise of miracles sustains shallow disciples, but it never satisfies them. The people were saying to Jesus, "Come on! Do a really big one!"

How big? Verse 31: "Our fathers ate the manna in the desert." Now we're getting to their real objective. "As it is written, 'He gave them bread from heaven to eat.'" They were getting irritated, so they said, "You think You're so great because You fed twenty thousand people once. Not bad. But Moses gave manna daily to millions for years! Can You top that? How can You be greater than Moses? You fed us one time, and Moses fed us for years." (Whoever was articulating this for the crowd was pretty sharp.)

Jesus' answer in John 6:32 was far superior to their question: "Then Jesus said to them, 'Most assuredly, I say to you, Moses did not give you the bread from heaven, but My Father gives you the true bread from heaven.'" He said, in effect, "FYI, Moses didn't produce that bread, he just directed the collection of it; and it was only manna," which must have been some sort of nutritious angel food cake. Jesus continued, "For the bread of God is He who comes down from heaven and gives life to the world" (v. 33).

Moses' bread was for physical nourishment, but Jesus was the bread of spiritual nourishment. Manna couldn't prevent death. The whole generation, including Moses, died in the wilderness. Manna was for Israel; Jesus was for the world. "Yes, I am greater than Moses, because the bread that I give will satisfy your soul." Verse 34: "Then they said to Him, 'Lord, give us this bread always.'" In other words, "Just keep giving it to us if it will end our hunger." They never got the point. All they wanted was to make demands and have Jesus meet them.

Now we get to the real issue. The crowd was pouring after Him, following Him, and He began to sort them out with the truth. The truth divides people. The more fundamental the truth, the deeper and wider the division. The goal of Christian preaching—the goal of presenting the gospel, the goal of the church—is not just to open the door so wide that we can suck everybody in and make them feel comfortable. The goal is to preach the truth to as many people as possible, so that we can sort out the true from the false.

## NO PERSONAL RELATIONSHIP

Spiritual defectors seek no personal relationship. John 6:36: "But I said to you that you have seen Me and yet do not believe." This is the beginning of a benchmark passage that also reads as a somewhat sad soliloquy. In verse 37, Jesus said, "All that the Father gives Me will come to Me." Why did He say that, all of a sudden? To whom was He talking? He had just told them that He was what they were look-ing for, the bread of heaven that gives eternal life to the world: "And Jesus said to them, 'I am the bread of life. He who comes to Me shall never hunger, and he who believes in Me shall never thirst'" (v. 35).

For any of us who go out to preach the gospel and proclaim the truth of Christ, for any who are brokenhearted and grieved over un-belief, we regain our hope on the solid promise that all whom the Father draws will come. This promise propelled Jesus into His state-ment in John 6:37–38: "All that the Father gives Me will come to Me, and the one who comes to Me I will by no means cast out. For I have come down from heaven, not to do My own will, but the will of Him who sent Me." He comforted Himself with the reminder that salvation was all the Father's plan anyway. And when the Father drew people to Him, they would come.

In verse 39, Jesus recognized that those people had absolutely no interest in a personal relationship with Him: "This is the will of the Father who sent Me, that of all He has given Me I should lose nothing, but should raise it up at the last day." Verse 40 sums it up:

"And this is the will of Him who sent Me, that everyone who sees the Son and believes in Him may have everlasting life; and I will raise him up at the last day." Jesus found His confidence, His balance in the midst of this tension between Himself and those defecting disciples by recalling the inviolable purposes of God that would ultimately come to pass.

## MUMBLING MOCKERS

Something else you inevitably will find true is that false Christians speak privately against the truth. When they're away from the true disciples, they mock the faith, either by what they say or how they live.

In John 6, they followed Jesus around, saying, "We want to make You King. Show us how to do Your works. Show us how to receive this eternal bread." But when they got away from that scene, what they said was very different. Verse 41: "The Jews then complained about Him, because He said, 'I am the bread which came down from heaven.'" They were—here's one of those interesting Greek words, *gonguzo*—complaining, murmuring, mumbling, grumbling, speaking clandestinely against Jesus.

When they were with the believers, they didn't do that. When they were with those who didn't believe, they mocked. Verse 42: "And they said, 'Is not this Jesus, the son of Joseph, whose father and mother we know? How is it then that He says, "I have come down from heaven"?'" They were making a joke of it. It would be very interesting to hear what people who are faithfully in church every Sunday say about religion in their conversations during the week, when unbelievers surround them. Do they defend the gospel, or do they mock it?

Jesus knew exactly what kind of mumbling and grumbling was going on. The people were mad because He had shattered their hope for free food. They had no interest in repentance or obedience or submission (which, by the way, is why you have to preach repentance, obedience, and submission). When they were away from Jesus and those close to Him, they jeered. No true lover of Jesus Christ would ever do that.

From that moment on, a remarkable thing happened. Instead of making the truth simpler in response to their mockery, Jesus began to make His message more difficult and hid the truth from them. He did this throughout His ministry, often by speaking in parables. He didn't argue or try to press His case; He simply returned to His confidence in God's sovereignty, as in John 6:44: "No one can come to Me unless the Father who sent Me draws him; and I will raise him up at the last day."

Evil trees can't bear good fruit, bitter fountains can't yield sweet water, and no one gets saved without a sovereign, gracious calling from God. Among true believers and ridiculing defectors alike, God will fulfill His saving purpose.

## DIVINE HUNGER

Defectors have no hunger for divine reality. John 6:45 says, "It is written in the prophets, 'And they shall all be taught by God.' Therefore everyone who has heard and learned from the Father comes to Me." Jesus was quoting from Isaiah 54:13 as a representative of the prophets, though Jeremiah, Joel, Micah, Zephaniah, and Malachi stated that same concept in their writings.

Jesus was affirming the great truth of the doctrine of election: when the Father chooses, the Father teaches; when the Father teaches, they learn; when they learn, they're drawn; when they're drawn, they come; when they come, Jesus receives them; when He receives them, He keeps them; when He keeps them, He raises them to eternal life. And then the Father's purpose is accomplished.

John 46–51:

> Not that anyone has seen the Father, except He who is from God; He has seen the Father. Most assuredly, I say to you, he who believes in Me has everlasting life. I am the bread of life. Your fathers ate the manna in the wilderness, and are dead. This is the bread which comes down from heaven, that one may eat of it and not die. I am the living bread which came down from heaven. If anyone eats of this bread, he will live forever; and the bread that I shall give is My flesh, which I shall give for the life of the world.

This was tremendous teaching from Jesus about salvation. He was saying, "The Father, whom you haven't seen, will draw you. If you will believe, you will have eternal life. I am the bread of life; it is Me you must believe in. And if you believe, you will never die, but live forever."

God promised salvation to all who believe in the person and work of Jesus Christ. But the mob didn't have any interest in that divine reality. They came around and sniffed a little, looked a little, admired a little, analyzed a little, philosophized a little, eulogized a little, and maybe even commended—a little. But that's all.

The key is in verse 51: "If anyone eats of this bread, he will live forever." But the crowd had no interest in eating anything spiritual. What the Scripture meant by eating was the personal appropriation by faith of Christ and His work: to have eternal life, you have to believe in Jesus Christ, that He died as a sacrifice for sin and arose from the dead as testimony to His power and the perfection of His sacrifice.

Jesus' listeners didn't respond by believing; they responded by arguing in verse 52: "The Jews therefore quarreled among themselves, saying, 'How can this Man give us His flesh to eat?'" They were saying, "This is ridiculous. What's He talking about, cannibalism? There's not enough of Him to go around." They knew He was talking about spiritual realities, but they were mocking Him again. They really had no interest in divine things. Spiritual defectors never do.

## GREAT CRY OF A THIRSTY SOUL

A final characteristic of Christian defectors is that they have no deeply felt hunger for forgiveness and deliverance from judgment.

Think for a moment about the rich young ruler in Matthew 19:16 who asked Jesus, "What do I do to get eternal life?" He didn't demonstrate a great hunger for salvation from sin, he just wanted to make sure he didn't miss eternal life. But he went away without salvation and deliverance from sin, because that's not what he really wanted. He didn't have a deep ache in his heart or recognize his spiritual hunger and thirst.

That's the point Jesus made, starting in John 6:53: "Then Jesus said to them, 'Most assuredly, I say to you, unless you eat the flesh of the Son of Man and drink His blood, you have no life in you.'"

Was He talking about a Catholic mass where somehow the bread and the cup are transubstantiated into the actual body and blood of Christ? Or about a Lutheran communion service in which the elements are somehow spiritually consubstantiated, comingled with the body and blood of Jesus Christ, in an actual eating of the very flesh and drinking of the very blood of Jesus?

Of course not! What He was simply saying was that eating the flesh of the Son of Man meant His hearers had to take into their minds and hearts the reality that God was incarnate in Jesus Christ. They had to fully embrace the reality of the Incarnation, and they had to take in the fact of His sacrificial death for sin. That's what drinking His blood meant. They needed to acknowledge that Jesus Christ was God in human flesh, and they had to personally appropriate the

reality of His righteous life and His substitutionary death, accepting
His perfect, sinless life and His shed blood as a sacrifice for sin.

Then John 6:54 says: Whoever eats My flesh and drinks My
blood has eternal life, and I will raise him up at the last day."

Here is the great cry for a hungry and thirsty soul, for His flesh
is the true food and His blood is the true drink. Continuing with
verses 55–58:

> For My flesh is food indeed, and My blood is drink indeed. He
> who eats My flesh and drinks My blood abides in Me, and I in
> him. As the living Father sent Me, and I live because of the Father,
> so he who feeds on Me will live because of Me. This is the bread
> which came down from heaven—not as your fathers ate the
> manna, and are dead. He who eats this bread will live forever.

Salvation is giving up your life and embracing His. It is taking in
Christ by faith, acknowledging the reality of who He is and what He
did. This is an invitation to receive Christ, and only the hungry eat;
only the thirsty drink. The spiritual traitor is not hungry for real salvation. He's not starving in sin and ravenous for righteousness. He's
full of the world and more than that, full of himself, satisfied, fed
with the prevailing food of the world that perishes. When someone
comes to Christ, he comes out of a driving spiritual hunger. As Jesus
said in the Sermon on the Mount, "Blessed are those who hunger and
thirst for righteousness, / For they shall be filled" (Matt. 5:6).

The image of eating illustrates graphically the personal appropriation of these realities. I can look at Christ and like what I see, but it's
no good unless I take it in. When a sinner loves his sin, is stuffed with
the world and happy with all the husks that he shares with the pigs,
he won't seek true salvation. To him, the thought of the bread of
Christ is ridiculous, repulsive, and nauseating, and he disdains it in
his self-satisfied bloatedness. He pushes Christ away.

But once a person is broken over sin, awakened to his lost condition and his purposelessness; once he senses the void and the gnawing hunger of his soul for God, then he cries out to be fed, takes Christ, and confesses Him as Lord and Savior. He says, "He's my life, He's my bread!" It's personal; there's no proxy. Each has to do it for himself. Christ gave His life for the world, but only those who come and eat receive that life.

## THE ONLY SOURCE

We come to the climax of the story, beginning in John 6:60: "Therefore many of His disciples, when they heard this, said, 'This is a hard saying; who can understand it?'" The word "disciples," *mathetes*, refers to learners or followers, not necessarily true believers. What they meant by "hard saying" was that it was offensive. They were complaining, "What He says is we don't have spiritual life, and He's the only source. If we're going to have spiritual life, we have to take Him. But He is repelling us, because He won't feed us breakfast and won't give us the power to feed ourselves. All He ever does is remind us of what we don't have and that He is everything. He won't say what we want the Messiah to say, and He refuses do what we want Him to do! We're not going to take this!"

Verse 61: "When Jesus knew in Himself that His disciples complained about this, He said to them, 'Does this offend you?'" Conscious that His disciples mocked again, He asked, "Does this news cause you to stumble? Don't you believe in Me as the Son of Man anymore?"

Verses 62–64: "What then if you should see the Son of Man ascend where He was before?" He was asking, "If I just take off right now, and go back into heaven, will you believe Me then?" Jesus continued, "'It is the Spirit who gives life; the flesh profits nothing. The words that I speak to you are spirit, and they are life. But there are some of you who do not believe.' For Jesus knew from the beginning who they were who did not believe, and who would betray Him."

The last thing they wanted was for Jesus to go back to heaven. How were they going to get free food if He left? They didn't need supernatural proof; they were stuck with their focus on their own selfish, earthly, material wants, and that's why they didn't hear Jesus' words or believe in Him. Jesus was omniscient. He already knew who the defectors were and who His betrayer would be. (By the way, Judas didn't leave with this group. He stayed all the way to the end, hoping he would eventually cash in on the Christ.)

John 6:65: "And He said, 'Therefore I have said to you that no one can come to Me unless it has been granted to him by My Father.'" This is a remarkable statement. Again Jesus relied on the sovereign plan of God to heal the pain of rejection. He felt the hurt, but He leaned confidently on the sovereignty of God, who will grant life to whomever He wills.

Finally, after all that, we come to verse 66: "From that time many of His disciples went back and walked with Him no more." He rested in the sovereignty of God, but that didn't ease the pain in His heart, as verse 67 shows: "Then Jesus said to the Twelve, 'Do you also want to go away?'" Jesus could weep over the city of Jerusalem, and He could be heartbroken over a rejection so penetrating that it could cause Him to feel a compelling loneliness. I think verse 67 reveals a brokenhearted Jesus. He suffered the real pain of rejection by these short-term disciples.

When Jesus asked, "Do you also want to go away?" there's real agony in that statement. Peter responded in verses 68–69: "But Simon Peter answered Him, 'Lord, to whom shall we go? You have the words of eternal life. Also we have come to believe and know that You are the Christ, the Son of the living God.'"[1]

It took us all the way to verse 68 of this chapter before we met a real disciple, except for the mention of the apostles who helped pass out the fishes and loaves. We finally find some real disciples who say, "We haven't got anywhere to go. You have the words of eternal life, and we have believed and come to know that You are the Holy One of God"—a messianic title. These were the ones who did think of heavenly things. They were the ones who genuinely desired a personal relationship with Jesus Christ, who understood His life, and who, with hearts broken over their sins, desired to repent and experience salvation. Bless them, because they comforted the Lord with their love and loyalty in that hour.

## A KISS OF BETRAYAL

But the chapter doesn't end with this encouraging note; it ends with the haunting reality of spiritual defection. John 6:70–71: "Jesus answered them, 'Did I not choose you, the twelve, and one of you is a devil?' He spoke of Judas Iscariot, the son of Simon, for it was he who would betray Him, being one of the twelve." He was the prototypical defector, one who stayed the longest, saw and heard the most, but never came to a place of commitment to Christ. Judas is the perfect closing illustration of the defector of whom Jesus said, "It would have been good for that man if he had not been born" (Matt. 26:24). Nonexistence is better than eternal hell.

Judas was drawn by the crowd. He was fascinated by the supernatural. He was thinking always of earthly things. He had no real desire to worship Christ; he sought only personal gain. He demanded what he wanted, and he made himself treasurer somehow and stole from the group's funds. He never had a true relationship with Christ, had no understanding of divine truth, no hunger for salvation. And Judas is not a solitary figure. Every church has its Judases, and millions of them have given Jesus a kiss of betrayal.

This is a heartbreaking realization. I hope and pray with all my heart that there is no Judas reading this page who, having defected from Jesus, will walk away into the darkest and bleakest night of severest eternal judgment.

I pray for any who are superficial, who are spiritual defectors, who will be traitors because they're attracted to Christ for all the wrong reasons. O God, may they see the need to worship the living Christ for who He is, to seek eternal things and not temporal things.

How much more seriously will they be judged who have known the truth and turned from it. I pray that in Your grace, You would save, before it's too late, any who have been deceived into thinking they're true believers without any passion for the worship of the God and Savior in whom they say they believe. Reveal the truth to every heart, and bring genuine conversion to those who are not yet genuine, lest the day come when, like the people in John 6:66, they walk no more with Him, and like Judas, they go to the place of everlasting judgment reserved for such traitors.

# 11

## WHY WE'RE STILL HERE

I believe every true Christian would agree that the gospel is the heart of Christianity, that we find it only in the Scripture, and that it must be preached to the ends of the earth. I grew up understanding that. My theological education affirmed it, and my years of studying the Bible have sealed that affirmation. The heart of the Christian faith is the gospel as found in the New Testament, whose foundations are in the Old Testament. And if it is going to save people, we must preach it throughout the world.

That is essentially the Christian mission, which the church has traditionally affirmed. Jesus said, "Go therefore and make disciples of all the nations, baptizing them in the name of the Father and of the Son and of the Holy Spirit, teaching them to observe all things that I have commanded you" (Matt. 28:19–20). He also said it another way: "Go into all the world and preach the gospel to every creature" (Mark 16:15).

True Christians have always believed that if people don't hear the gospel, they can't be saved, and that they will consequently spend eternity in hell under the judgment of God. So it's absolutely critical that the world not only hear the gospel of Jesus Christ, but that people understand it accurately and believe it absolutely.

Compelled by this clear biblical mandate, Christians through the centuries have taken the saving message of the gospel to the ends of the earth. It's the only reason we're still here. True Christians are already saved and sealed for eternity. There's no reason to leave us on earth, except for this responsibility of evangelism.

The Bible clearly tells us that salvation comes through believing in Christ, which, in turn, comes from hearing and understanding the gospel. That can occur only if somebody takes the message into the world. And somebody can take the message only if someone sends it. Romans 10 teaches us that believing in Christ saves us, but we can't believe in Christ unless we hear about Him (vv. 9, 14). Therefore, telling others about Christ has been our mandate and mission since the church was born on Pentecost, when Jesus said, "You'll receive the Holy Spirit, and you'll be witnesses unto Me in Jerusalem, Judea, Samaria, and the uttermost part of the earth" (see Acts 1:8).

From the time Jesus launched the church until today, taking the only message of salvation to the ends of the earth has required the sacrifice of uncounted millions of dollars in every currency in the world, millions of hours of effort, and millions of Christian people's energies. Part of that has been the rigorous, difficult, challenging work of learning a language with no written form, developing an alphabet and writing system, then teaching the people to read their own language, giving them the Scriptures, and leading them to Christ. This can take decades, but it's part of an unrelenting effort to use every means available to reach people with the one message that can save them from eternal judgment: the gospel of Jesus Christ.

Along with my family, I got a renewed appreciation and respect for missionary work a few years ago, on a trip to Hong Kong. The underground church in China had requested copies of some Christian books and Bibles that have been translated into Chinese, and I was asked if my family and I would help smuggle them into the country.

My wife and our four teenage children huddled in our hotel

room as I explained the plan. "Kids, we've been given an assignment to smuggle books into China. We'll pick them up here in Hong Kong, hide them in our luggage, and sneak them over the border. Once we get across, we leave them at a prearranged secret drop point, and someone from the church will pick them up after we're gone."

The kids started jumping around, thinking they were all going to be Indiana Jones. I said, "Now, we might get through the border crossing without being searched. You've got to keep your cool. If they do go through our stuff and find the books, they'll confiscate them—and we pray that's all they'll do." Still, everybody gave the plan an enthusiastic thumbs-up.

The kids filled their duffel bags with books and stuffed more in their shirts. We blasted out of Hong Kong across the China Sea on a jet hydrofoil, and in a couple of hours we arrived in Macao. I paused long enough to take them to the grave of Robert Morrison, the great Chinese missionary, and we wept and prayed over his grave to honor his giving his life to take the gospel to these people.

We went through border security, and through the providences of God, they didn't search anybody. No sooner did they get past the last guard than all four children took off running like scared rabbits, as hard and fast as they could! We took a taxi to a cemetery. In the middle of the cemetery was a little building with a broken window. As we'd been instructed to do, we took turns climbing up on a headstone and dumping our books through the broken window.

For my children to really experience a taste of the lives of suffering believers in another part of the world, and to be able to make a small contribution in that way, was a wonderful lesson. It's important for every Christian to be reminded of those countless selfless people, many of them lost to history, who have made immense sacrifices around the world for the cause of Christ.

## NEW MEDIA, TIMELESS MESSAGE

Twenty-first-century communications technology has given us greater power than ever to bring the timeless truth of the gospel to the ends of the earth. The pace of change is ever faster. It took a generation to go from the telegraph to the telephone, and another generation to go from the telephone to radio; now advances in the Internet and satellite communications seem to appear almost every day.

I've experienced firsthand how modern media can multiply a preacher's audience. Earlier we saw how, back in the 1800s, Henry Martyn traveled more than a thousand miles by mule to get the gospel message out in Persia. I probably spoke to as many people in the first few months of my ministry as he reached after all those months on a mule in the desert, not because I made any great personal sacrifice, but because I had electronic technology.

When I was a seminary student, my dad preached on a television program called *The Voice of Calvary*. Every Sunday night after church, he and I jumped in the car and raced down to the studio for a live television broadcast on what is now the UPN network. My first real preaching exposure came when I took my dad's place once in a while on live TV. I wasn't sure I was ready, but my dad felt it was a great opportunity. Nobody listened to me in the studio; technicians, musicians waiting for their cue, and other busy and preoccupied people went about their business. Yet standing there in front of a camera, I felt the sense that through the unprecedented reach of television, I could introduce the gospel to people I couldn't even see.

The impact of modern communication on sharing the gospel of Christ really hit me the first time I ever went to the Philippines. Though I'd never been there before, my sermons had played on the radio for years as part of my *Grace to You* radio ministry. So they knew me, but I didn't know them.

I was invited to preach in Manila at the Philippine Intercultural Conference Center, the country's largest meeting venue. It seated five thousand people, and I wondered why in the world I'd be preaching there, since I didn't expect that many people to know who I was. I'll never forget walking in and not only finding five thousand seats filled, but more people standing around the perimeter of the room. And I thought, "Wow, how could this happen?"

It demonstrated to me, as nothing else could, the power of teaching God's Word on radio. When the service was over, the mob of people wanting me to sign books (ones they had ordered through the radio ministry) crushed me. I was overwhelmed. It was a phenomenal insight for me to realize how personal radio is, and how effectively it helps bring the gospel.

## FUZZY FAITH FAILS

It should come as no surprise that, at this point in time, the enemy of men's souls—God's archenemy, Satan himself—has cranked up his efforts to prevent the spread of the gospel. One of his prime tactics is to make the church confused about what the gospel is. It doesn't do any good to have this fantastic contemporary communication technology, or wealth, manpower, and passion to take the gospel message to the ends of the earth, if you don't know what the gospel message is. So it's certainly a wise strategy on the part of the enemy of men's souls to confuse the church about the message.

Along with many others, I've been preaching, teaching, and writing to try and clarify for Christians what the gospel is. They're not really sure whether Jesus is Lord or not, or whether He *needs* to be Lord or not. It doesn't seem to be important these days that people understand the true biblical doctrine of justification by faith alone, through grace alone, in Christ alone. It doesn't seem to matter to some people that there be repentance of sin, and that we preach repentance. In fact, some people think the idea of repentance is an intrusion into grace. They fail to comprehend the doctrine of substitution and imputation, which is the true understanding that God imputed (meaning ascribed or assigned) our sins fully to a substitute who died in our place, and that we contribute nothing to our salvation but lay hold of eternal life by faith in that substitute.

In spite of the absolute clarity of the gospel, even so-called evangelicals can end up with a fuzzy view of their faith because of all the confusion in the air. I've heard the pastor of a very large evangelistic church claim, "The Reformation was overrated as to its importance." No. What the Reformation did was define the gospel and rescue it from its corrupters. Not only do we seem unsure what the gospel is sometimes, we're not even convinced it's important to get it right. That is a tragic mistake. Here we are, with all this awesome potential to spread the gospel to the ends of the earth, and we're not sure what the gospel is!

In the process of stewing about the issue, the church has gotten shallower and shallower. One reason is because churches have proliferated everywhere in which the pastors are personality-driven leaders, men who don't have the theological grounding to define issues biblically with any depth. Another reason is this tragic and misguided concern not to offend anybody, to make church fun and entertaining, resulting in some kind of synthetic gospel that doesn't have enough truth in it to save anybody.

All of that is bad enough, but there's a new wave in the evangelical world that is at least as frightening, if not more: the theory that it isn't necessary to take the gospel to the ends of the earth, because people are being saved without it.

This view has several labels that we can examine by veering off into a little theology class for a minute. One name for it is *natural theology*, the notion that somebody can get to heaven without the gospel. It holds that mankind can ascend naturally to a knowledge of God and a relationship with Him by virtue of his reason and innate desire to obey God's will. This is a natural, as opposed to supernatural, approach.

*Supernatural theology* says God has to come down and save man. Natural theology says man can climb up to God, thanks to a natural reasoning process, and that the Scripture is unnecessary. Advocates of this view say mankind may discover the basic existence, attributes, and nature of God by human reason, apart from scriptural revelation, and attain to a saving knowledge of God.

If you believe that, you obviously could not have a reformed view of depravity. You would have to believe that man has not only innate reasoning power, but innate goodness to pursue righteousness. Therefore, people who advocate natural theology have a flawed view of man's depravity. Their point of view is that man can make it to heaven without the Bible, so what's all the missionary fuss about? You don't need repentance toward God and faith in Jesus Christ, as Paul said he had to preach in Acts 20:21. This view holds that the lost don't need to hear the gospel. They don't need to have Bibles. Apparently, we don't need all these people such as Robert Morrison and Henry Martyn sacrificing their lives in remote areas with isolated populations, trying to translate the Bible for them, because they can be saved without it.

Even as historic and influential a body as the Catholic church believes people can be saved without the gospel, as a story in the *Los Angeles Times* showed. The newspaper quoted Pope John Paul II saying, "All who live a just life will be saved, even if they do not believe in Jesus Christ and the Roman Catholic Church." The pope continued, "The gospel teaches us that those who live in accordance with the Beatitudes, poor in spirit, the pure in heart, those who bear lovingly the sufferings of life, will enter God's Kingdom."[1]

The pope is taking an inclusive view of salvation. Many people reject the biblical teaching that salvation comes only in response to faith in Jesus Christ. They insist that the heathen are saved if they just live good lives—if they're poor in spirit, pure in heart, and do what's right. As long as they are sincere, what they believe doesn't really matter.

This has been in the fabric of Roman Catholicism for centuries. That is why Catholic apologist Peter Kreeft, who wrote the book *Ecumenical Jihad*, can say that there are Buddhists, Hindus, Confucianists, Muslims, atheists, and orthodox Jews in heaven: sincerity and goodness are the ticket to God's kingdom, not believing in the Christ of the gospel. Through innate goodness, they naturally reason themselves into a knowledge of God, please Him, and earn their salvation, whether they ever set eyes on a Bible in their lives or not.[2] The pope, in his comment, simply affirmed what many Catholic theologians have long believed.

## REDEFINING MERCY AND MISSIONS

The evangelical counterpart to natural theology is known as the "wider mercy" view. Natural theology claims that man, even in his depraved condition, can find God on his own—a view impossible to substantiate with Scripture. Self-proclaimed evangelicals, rather than posture themselves as natural theologians, come up with another title, the wider mercy concept, which lets them remain true to supernatural theology by insisting there's this wider latitude, this inclusive view, in which the Lord is going to include everybody. It says any religion can save people.

An oft-quoted saying goes like this:

When we approach the man of another faith than our own it will be in a spirit of expectancy to find how God has been speaking to him and what new understanding of the grace and love of God we may ourselves discover in this encounter. Our first task in approaching another people, another culture, another religion, is to take off our shoes, for the place we are approaching is holy. Else we may find ourselves treading on men's dreams. More serious still, we may forget that God was here before our arrival.[3]

The frightening reality is that evangelicals are beginning to echo that language and say similar things. This redefines the whole concept of missions. Instead of going into a tribe and saying that those people are lost, doomed, and in darkness, you should say you're standing on holy ground, because God has been there in the form of their paganism!

I cannot imagine a more disastrous belief than that. "God has more going on by way of redemption than what happened in first century Palestine"? This says that the life and death and resurrection of Jesus Christ formed just one chain of events in the midst of many, rather than the single greatest event in all redemptive history. That depreciates Christ, His virgin birth, His incarnation, His sinless life, His substitutionary death, His bodily resurrection, His ascension, His intercession, the Second Coming . . . everything!

This is a regurgitation of an old Greek heresy that the apostle John dealt with called the "universal logos," where Christ's Spirit is floating around, injecting Himself into every religion. Such views also attack the Trinity, because only biblical Christianity affirms that God is a Trinity. Mormons also deny this.

How can people believe in a wider mercy, when the Bible says salvation is in Christ alone? In John 14:6, Jesus said, "I am the way, the truth and the life. No man comes to the Father except through Me." Pretty clear. Acts 4:12: "Nor is there salvation in any other, for there is no other name under heaven given among men by which we must be saved." Jesus said in John 8, "Because you believe not in Me, you'll die in your sins, and where I go, you'll never come."

Anybody who reads the New Testament has to know that believing in Jesus is the only way to be saved. There's only "one Mediator between God and men, the Man Christ Jesus" (1 Tim. 2:5). How do proponents of these other theologies deal with this? Some of them talk about Jesus every time they're on television. But to say, first, that Jesus is the only Savior, and then to say Muslims, Buddhists, animists, and who-knows-what are also going to be in the body of Christ and in the kingdom of heaven—how does that work?

Some who hold this view agree that the work of Christ is the only basis of salvation, but they insist it isn't necessary to know that in order to be saved. In other words, if you believe in God—however you imagine God to be—and if you try to do what's right, good, and "religious," Christ is going to save you, even though you didn't know who He was or what He did. Even though you didn't know God was a Trinity, or that He revealed Himself in Christ, who lived and died and rose again, Christ is still going to be your Savior and atone for your sins.

## A VISIT WITH MOTHER TERESA

Several years ago my family and I had the opportunity to visit Mother Teresa in Calcutta, and I gave her a copy of my book *The Gospel According to Jesus*. This very strong, very gracious, very self-less little woman said she would read it, but Mother Teresa was true to her Catholic faith. In the front of a Bible that she autographed for a young man who had also met her, she wrote, "May you enter into the heart of Jesus through the Virgin Mary." So she believed that salvation comes by virtue of Mary.

When we went into her home for the sick and dying in Calcutta, I was surprised to see pictures of those bizarre multiarmed Hindu gods on the walls of that Catholic facility. I wondered how she could post pictures of Hindu gods that were associated with a Hindu sacrificial temple right next door; there, vile, wrenchingly deviant blood sacrifices were made from oxen and other creatures. I just assumed that this was political correctness, and that if she were going to survive in the city of Calcutta, she had to defer to the political rulers. Later I came to understand that this was a part of the direction modern Roman Catholic theology is moving, led by the pope.

One author claims that good Hindus are saved by Christ and not by Hinduism. Through the sacraments of Hinduism, through the message of morality and the good life, through the mysticism that comes down to them through Hinduism Christ, saves them, according to this view."

Everybody's in! Good Hindus, good Buddhists, good people you see on the Discovery Channel, running around with bones through their lips: they're all in the kingdom, as long as they're good. This is an unfathomable belief to have intruded into evangelicalism. I could understand if it were coming out of some liberal seminary or an apostate denomination that overtly rejects the Bible. But knowing the people who are endorsing this, people in churches who say they believe the Bible, I am deeply disappointed.

How could we succumb to this? How could pastors be saying that the Reformation doesn't really matter, and maybe we really need to redefine missions altogether?

## THE CASE FOR EXCLUSIVISM

We have a major problem here. And the only way to deal with this all-important issue is simply to go to the Scriptures. I'm not going to give you my opinion, because my opinion isn't worth anything. God's Word is the only thing that counts, and it counts for everything. Is there a biblical case for exclusivism, the idea that if you don't know the gospel, and if you don't believe in Jesus Christ, you aren't going to heaven?

The answer is yes. There is an *overwhelming* case for exclusivism. We've been making it all through this book. And we also have a biblical case for the fact that natural theology isn't going to get anybody anywhere. We've already seen in Matthew 7 that God's mercy is extremely narrow, and that those who would be saved have to enter through the narrow gate.

It all starts with the story of the fall of man in Genesis 3. Up to this point in the Bible, Adam and Eve were in a condition of perfection, living in an earthly paradise known as the Garden of Eden. Though they had perfect minds, Adam and Eve couldn't understand on their own why they were created. They could understand that they were created, and that something more powerful than they created them—some immense Being who loved beauty and order and design and gave them life. But they couldn't understand why they were created unless somebody told them.

God said to them, "You can eat everything." Otherwise they wouldn't have known that. And He said, "Don't eat that. If you do, you'll die." And He said, "This is your wife: have babies." And He said, "Name those animals." That's why they walked and talked with God in the garden, because God gave them special revelation about how they were to relate to Him and to their world.

Natural theologians should be shocked to discover that Adam couldn't know divine truth by his perfect reason! By his own reason, his own perfect intellect, he couldn't have come to know that he was to eat this and not to eat that, that he was to name the animals, tend the garden, and so forth. God had to tell him all of that information. He didn't naturally know it. *God* was the origin and source of truth, justice, morals, meaning, and beauty. Man was not the origin of truth, but the receiver of truth.

It's true. Adam and Eve would have known something about God, but they wouldn't have known what God wanted from them if He hadn't told them. You can study all the religions, philosophers, and theologians of the world, and none of them ever comes up with the right understanding of man's creation and man's depravity. You can't get there from depraved natural reasoning.

When Satan got into that perfect garden with that perfect man and woman, he told them to distrust God's instruction and rely on their own reason. That's what he still wants in the world today. After a little chat with Eve, he finally said to her, "You're not going to die. You can't believe God—God lies. He said you're going to die? Don't believe it. You're not going to die, you're going to be like God. He just doesn't like the competition!" Satan tempted man to trust his own natural reason and reject supernatural revelation from the mouth of God.

God gave them special revelation: "Don't eat." Satan countered, "Don't believe what God says. Trust your reason!" That's essentially what natural theology claims. It's just that same old satanic lie: "You can get there through your reason. Don't worry about the Bible. Don't worry about the gospel. You don't need them."

So, how could fallen man, in a cursed world, find God's truth by his perverted reason, when perfect man in a perfect world couldn't find God with perfect reason? Even Adam couldn't know what God wanted if God didn't tell him, and nobody else can know what God wants if God doesn't tell him.

Satan always wants to depreciate the special revelation. What a great strategy it is to say, "Let's convince the church it doesn't even need to preach the gospel." Tell me where that heresy came from—heaven? Here's a hint: who has the most to gain if we stop preaching the gospel?

## THE CLEAR TRUTH OF CREATIONISM

Romans 1:18–23 gives us a clear lesson in biblical anthropology:

> For the wrath of God is revealed from heaven against all ungodliness and unrighteousness of men, who suppress the truth in unrighteousness, because what may be known of God is manifest in them, for God has shown it to them. For since the creation of the world His invisible attributes are clearly seen, being understood by the things that are made, even His eternal power and Godhead, so that they are without excuse, because, although they knew God, they did not glorify Him as God, nor were thankful, but became futile in their thoughts, and their foolish hearts were darkened. Professing to be wise, they became fools, and changed the glory of the incorruptible God into an image made like the corruptible man—and birds and four-footed animals and creeping things.

The Bible says here that there is evidence about God (v. 19). What is known about God is evident through reason. Reason looks at creation (v. 20) and says, "There must be a Creator." Reason looks at the diversity and says, "He must have an immense mind." It looks at the design and says, "He's a God of order." It looks at the beauty and says, "He's a God of beauty and harmony." It looks at vast variety and says, "He's a God of incredible power and complexity."

Yes, that's all true. So true, in fact, that God's eternal power and divine nature are visible through reason looking at creation. You simply can't look at the results of creation and doubt there's a Creator. You'd have to commit intellectual suicide to deny there is a cause for the effect of the universe, that there is a supreme Maker. The end of verse 20—"His invisible attributes are clearly seen, being understood by the things that are made, even His eternal power and

Godhead, so that they are without excuse"—makes this so clear that people have absolutely no excuse for being evolutionists. None. It is absolute idiocy. Paul used *moria*, the Greek term for "moron," translated "fool" or "foolish." Any rational, thinking person, who sees anything that exists, assumes somebody made it. And the universe certainly demands a Creator.

Paul said God has given man reason, and reason looks at creation and concludes certain things about the power and nature of the Creator. And he's without excuse. The problem is, that doesn't lead him to God because, as verse 18 warned, men "suppress the truth in unrighteousness." Man is so wicked, vile, and ungodly that his depravity negates the possibility of his coming all the way to God on his own natural powers. Instead, he suppresses the truth. He dishonors the Creator even though the knowledge of God as Creator is obvious around Him.

Verse 21 says the people would not glorify or honor God. Man turns away from God, suppressing the truth and replacing it with empty speculation. That's how supposedly smart people come up with stupid lies like evolution. They invent human ideas that are not reality, and their foolish hearts go dark.

They end up with nothing but garbled understanding in their egotism, as Romans 1:22 states, which is a major part of depravity. They profess to be wise, give themselves Ph.D.s, put on royal and religious robes and cone hats, and march around as if they're some great religious wise men. They are fools. They are morons.

Verse 23: They have "changed the glory of the incorruptible God into an image made like corruptible man"—animals and birds and bugs. They make gods out of other things. Natural man worships creatures. His reason says there must be a God, but because of his wicked love of sin, he suppresses that truth. He can't help but do so, because he doesn't have any path to God. These people are dead in trespasses and sins. In that deadness, truth and righteousness are repressed, and in their place comes the fabrication of false religious systems and silly philosophies.

According to verse 18, the end of all human philosophy and religion is "the wrath of God." That's the whole point. These verses drive home the truth that natural man, with his natural theology, unaided by special revelation, winds up inexcusably under divine judgment. He can expect the wrath of God, not the grace of God. You can't visit some tribe that's worshipping an alligator and say, "Oh, I'm on holy ground. God was here before I arrived!" God was not there. God is not there. That is not truth. That is a refusal to honor the true and living God, and an attempt to put something else in His place—some hollow philosophy, foolish religion, or lifeless idol. And the end result is judgment and hell.

A man who attains the highest level of religious pride, the one who chooses his own god, is a moron and a fool. First Corinthians 1:18 gives us a reinforcing image of that thought: "For the message of the cross is foolishness to those who are perishing, but to us who are being saved it is the power of God." Fools think the biblical truth is foolish; those who are saved recognize its power.

In verse 19 Paul quotes another judgment from Isaiah 29:14 (NAS): "For it is written, 'I will destroy the wisdom of the wise and the cleverness of the clever I will set aside.'" Both "destroy" and "set aside" speak of a sort of final judgment, an execution. God says, "Go ahead: line up the wisest of the wise, the cleverest of the clever, and I'll cut them down."

It's comforting and encouraging to know we have a powerful protector against all comers. The idea reminds me of my school friend Roger. The rough crowd—the guys who shaved and drove cars to school even though they were still in the eighth grade—teased Roger and me a lot. They came up behind us and punched all the books out from under our arms, or smashed our heads against the lockers.

One day, after they'd pounded us for something, Roger said, "I've had it. I'm going to tell my brother." His brother was a middle linebacker for Long Beach State and a weight lifter. He had once driven a bread truck into a stone wall and walked away.

The next morning, Roger and I went to the area outside the gym, where these tough guys hung out before school. Roger said something to them, and when they started laughing, his brother came around the corner and asked, "Which one of these guys is bugging you the most?"

Roger pointed to a boy and said, "That one!" The guy stopped laughing and froze in his tracks. Roger's brother calmly picked him up by the throat and threw him over a hedge, then said, "I don't want anybody ever to touch Roger again." And they didn't. Roger ruled the school from then on. That display of indomitable power changed everything. And for me, ever since, it's been an unforgettable illustration of the sure and absolute protection the Lord provides for His own against the enemy, however he comes, whatever form he assumes. *I'm* not more powerful than the enemy of my soul, but I have a spiritual elder Brother, and the enemy trembles at His power.

Take the wisest of the wise, take the wisdom of the world, take the elite religious leaders, the people at the top echelons of their religion—from the pope or the leader of Hinduism or the Muslim world to the apostles in the Mormon church, all who have reached the epitome of man's devised schemes of religion—the wise, the great writers and theologians, the people who can argue their points on talk radio and win the day: God is going to unmask all those people as fools when it comes to spiritual truth.

He's going to cut them all down. The reason is in 1 Corinthians 1:21: the world, through its wisdom, did not come to know God. You can't get there from here. The world at its best, at its highest point of religious and intellectual achievement, cannot come to know God. That's not my opinion. That's what the Bible says.

The end of verse 21 reads, "It pleased God through the fool-ishness of the message preached to save those who believe." It points back to the "message of the cross" in verse 18. The only way you're going to get saved is by believing the message of the cross. It was God's plan that the world, through its wisdom, could never come to know Him. But God was pleased, through the foolishness of the cross, to save those who believe. You can't believe in any-thing you want to; you have to believe in that. And the gospel of the cross is not a product of human reason; it's the revelation in Scripture.

Satan loves to come into the garden today, pull people over, and say, "You don't really think you should believe what special revelation from God says! Trust your own reason!" That's what these wider mercy theologians are doing. They're just following Satan. Only the message of the cross can save. Anything else is insufficient folly.

If you reject Jesus Christ, you can't get to God. And you're never going to get to Him until you obediently hear and believe the mes-sage. That's why, for two thousand years, people have been going to the ends of the earth with the gospel of Christ: this is what we know the Bible teaches. Natural man, left to himself, ends up under the wrath of God.

Be faithful to share the gospel with everybody who comes across your path, sure in the knowledge that there is no other way to heaven except through the message of Jesus Christ and His cross.

# 12

## BUT SOME WILL BELIEVE

C hristianity would be much easier to sell if only it had a good dose of twenty-first-century inclusivism. On one level, the message of the Bible sounds so attractive and comforting: God is love! Jesus forgives your sins! That's terrific. The same gospel that tells us those things, though, also tells us to worship Jesus as Lord, that we can't earn our way to heaven, and that the only way to eternal life is through Christ.

We've seen that the frequent solution for making the message more popular and appealing is to distort and misrepresent the gospel by pumping up the easy parts and downplaying or ignoring the hard parts. We've also seen that many religious leaders around the world, including some who consider themselves evangelicals, take the question a step further by wondering aloud if people really need to have the gospel to be saved. Can't they get to heaven without it? Won't a multiarmed Hindu god or an alligator do in a pinch? And what about the people who never had the chance to hear the gospel? Sending them to hell is hardly fair!

There are two answers to these questions. First, you and I had better get to people with the gospel, because that's what God commanded us to do. Second, if God, in His sovereign, eternal, elective purpose, has determined to bring people to salvation, then He will be sure that they receive the gospel. Jesus said in the Sermon on the Mount, "Seek, and you will find" (Matt. 7:7). And we are the instruments that proclaim the gospel.

Whether or not the gospel is necessary for salvation is at the core of Christianity. The question is ultimately simple and straightforward: Either we can understand the Spirit and intentions of God on our own, or we cannot. And if we can't, we have to look at the only place in creation where the deeper essence of God is revealed: the Bible.

## SPIRIT BENEATH THE SURFACE

The last part of 1 Corinthians 2:10 says, "The Spirit searches all things, yes, the deep things of God." As deep and inaccessible as God is, we can still know some things about Him. He is powerful, He is complex, He's a God of order and beauty and life. It's true that we can see a lot in the creation. But if we want to go beneath the surface, to the spiritual side of God—to the law, the salvation, the righteousness, and the redemption of God—we have to perceive that the Spirit of God knows the deep things, because the Spirit is God.

In our human wisdom, we don't have access to the deep things; we have access only to what we can see on the surface. We don't know spiritual things about God: His nature, essence, will, and salvation.

Paul gave an analogy in 1 Corinthians 2:11: "For what man knows the things of a man except the spirit of the man which is in him?" We can be close to each other in the same family, or engaged in a common enterprise, yet we still can't know each other's thoughts. All we know is what is apparent to our senses. The only one who perfectly knows the thoughts is the spirit of the person who has the thoughts. The same is true of God. We can understand some things about Him from seeing what He has made, but none of us can know the deep things of God any more than I can know, by looking at you, what your innermost thoughts are. Only your spirit knows what's inside you, and only the Spirit of God knows the deep things of God.

We'll never know the deep, saving, spiritual truths of God unless someone reveals them to us. As 1 Corinthians 2:11 says, "No one knows the things of God except the Spirit of God." Paul added in verse 12, "Now we have received, not the spirit of the world, but the Spirit who is from God, that we might know the things that have been freely given to us by God." Those things are forgiveness of sin, salvation, and the hope of eternal life, as well as all the blessings of justification, sanctification, glorification. We can't know them by human reason. We can't find them in a test-tube experiment. We can't figure them out by rationalization. We can know them only through the revelation of the Holy Spirit.

You can't go to heaven unless you know how, and you can't know how except by reading the Bible. That's the only place where men wrote down words the Holy Spirit inspired. All Scripture is given by inspiration of God. Peter described the process: "holy men of God spoke as they were moved by the holy spirit" (2 Pet. 1:21).

This is going to come as a radical shock to those advocating natural theology. Imagine what they're going to say when they have 1 Corinthians 2:14 dropped in front of them: "But the natural man does not receive the things of the Spirit of God, for they are foolishness to him; nor can he know them, because they are spiritually discerned." A natural man, who lacks the aid of supernatural revelation through Scripture, cannot know the things that only the Spirit of God knows. To him, they are complete nonsense. He can't understand them because they are spiritually, not rationally, appraised. He can't examine them by empirical study; he can't attain them by any human intuition.

Where does natural theology lead you? Nowhere but hell. It is a fatal, dead-end street, entered through the wide gate that seems so comfortable, convenient, user-friendly, and seeker-sensitive. You can't understand the things of God on your own, any more than Adam and Eve could, because you can appraise the essence of the Lord and Creator of the universe only through the power and revelation of the Holy Spirit. Without the Spirit, there is no knowledge. But for those of us whom the Holy Spirit has taught through the Scriptures, we have what 1 Corinthians 2:16 calls "the mind of Christ."

We can know what Christ thinks because the Scriptures reveal it. Natural man, lacking the mind of Christ revealed through the Spirit, ends up with no understanding. He ends up a fool. And he ends up in judgment. In John 14:26, Jesus said to the disciples, "But the Helper, the Holy Spirit, whom the Father will send in My name, He will teach you all things, and bring to your remembrance all things that I said to you." He assured them that God would instruct them how to record the deep things that are not discernible to the human senses, the profound issues of salvation that constitute the mind of Christ.

## THE UNKNOWN GOD REVEALED

I have had the privilege of preaching a couple of times in the Areopagus near Mars Hill, just below the Parthenon in the center of Athens, where proponents of the false religions of the Greek Empire worshipped. Mars Hill is where the philosophers assembled in ancient times, and people gathered around to listen to them. It's a magnificent place, not only because of its history, but because of its beautiful location on the Acropolis.

Every time I walk there, I imagine Paul stepping onto the same stones, in the shadow of a massive pagan temple to Athena with other pagan temples all around him, and figuratively wiping it all away with the glory and truth of the one true God. I've delivered his sermon from Acts 17, standing on the spot where he preached it. Looking around at the broken columns and fallen walls, I can imagine an ancient marketplace filled with people and a crowd of intellectuals gathered to hear what this outsider had to say. That pagan world is nothing but rubble now, but the message of salvation is timeless and eternal.

Acts 17 describes Paul's visit to the Areopagus. The Epicureans, Stoics, and other philosophers invited him to address them, "For you are bringing some strange things to our ears. Therefore we want to know what these things mean" (v. 20).

No doubt the teachings of Christ were strange to this audience. Epicureans believed that the chief end of man was to avoid pain. They didn't deny the existence of God but believed He had no involvement with the earthly affairs of men; when a person died, his body and soul disintegrated. Stoics taught that the chief end of man was to master himself to the point that he was indifferent to pleasure or pain.

Accepting their invitation, Paul stood in the midst of the Areopagus and addressed the assembled group in verse 22: "Men of Athens, I perceive that in all things you are very religious." To some audiences or congregations today, that's the gospel in a nutshell: be very "religious" in all respects and assume God will count that as a fair-enough commitment, even if they don't know anything else. But Paul continued, "For as I was passing through and considering the objects of your worship, I even found an altar with this inscription: 'TO THE UNKNOWN GOD.'"

How interesting. They had many altars there to the pantheon of gods they worshipped, but they had this feeling there might be one left out, and they didn't want to offend him. To be on the safe side and remove any unnecessary offense, they put up an altar to the unknown god. Seeing that, Paul said to them, in essence, "This is a very religious thing to do. You don't know God, you haven't had

His revelation, you don't have the Old Testament, you don't know about the God who is the Creator, the God who is the Sustainer of the universe, the God who is the God of Abraham, Isaac, and Jacob, the God of Israel, the living and true God and Father of the Lord Jesus Christ. You reflect the problem of not having a supernatural revelation."

In verse 23 he explained, "Therefore, the One whom you worship without knowing, Him I proclaim to you." There they were, having achieved their epitome of philosophy and religion, and they were as ignorant as ignorant could be. So Paul said, "Let me tell you ignorant people who this unknown god of yours really is."

Paul realized that they didn't know God, and he wanted them to realize it too. He said, "Let me introduce Him to you. He's the God who made the world and all things in it. Since He is the Lord and Sovereign of heaven and earth, He doesn't dwell in temples made with hands, neither is He served by human hands. You don't put a wreath around His neck. You don't make some kind of offering to Him. That's not the kind of God He is. He doesn't need anything. You don't have to feed Him. You don't have to put flowers on Him. He Himself gives to all life and breath and all things."

Acts 17:26: "And He has made from one blood every nation of men to dwell on all the face of the earth, and has determined their preappointed times and the boundaries of their dwellings." In other words, "This is some God—the God of gods! This is the Creator of all in earth and in heaven. This is the eternal Spirit being, whom we can't confine to any kind of temple. He is the God who determines what nations exist, when and where they exist, and when they fade from the scene. He is the Writer and Determiner of history."

Then Paul added in verses 27–28, "He is not far from each one of us; for in Him we live and move and have our being." Do you know how close God is to a pagan? He's so close that He's there. No pagan would take another breath if God weren't there. Yet those on

Mars Hill still didn't know Him; they were still searching in igno-rance, though He was right inside them. One of their heathen poets even recognized, in verse 28, that "we are also His offspring."

Before the theory of evolution became popular, no one had this stupid thought that nobody times nothing equals everything. Before then, no one could come up with a proposal so ridiculous as the idea that everything came out of nothing. Every rational person understood that every effect had a cause, therefore, a Creator had to exist—a personal and moral Creator, because we're persons who understand moral law.

Acts 17:29: "Therefore, since we are the offspring of God, we ought not to think that the Divine Nature is like gold or silver or stone, something shaped by art and man's devising." Even their pagan reason told them there had to be a Creator. They were seek-ing truth; God was near, but instead of coming to know the true God, they made an idol. This reinforces the thought in Romans 1: they do it because, by their natural theology, they cannot understand God, nor the things of the Spirit of God. The philosophers of Athens hadn't done God any favors; they had just turned Him into a stone thing called the Unknown God. That's not God.

Verses 30–31 say, "Truly, these times of ignorance God over-looked, but now commands all men everywhere to repent, because He has appointed a day on which He will judge the world in righ-teousness by the Man whom He has ordained." Paul was not talking about repenting of those categorical sins that we usually associate with repentance; he was saying they had better turn completely away from—"repent" means to turn 180 degrees and go the opposite direction—false religion and head in the right direction. God had set a day when He would judge the world in righteousness, and He would use a Judge whom He already identified in John 5 as Jesus. He had proved to all men that Christ was the Judge by raising Him from the dead.

Some of Paul's listeners began to dismiss him, but others said, "We will hear you again on this matter" (Acts 17:32). They wanted more. And by the grace of God, "some men joined him and believed, among them Dionysius the Areopagite, a woman named Damaris, and others with them" (v. 34).

Here's a scriptural example of a true Christian who went to the pagans and said, "You're very religious, and you know there's a God, *but* you don't have the Bible [spiritual revelation], so you don't have the gospel or hope of eternal life." He didn't say, "Don't worry about it, guys, it's no big deal." Instead he told them, "You had better repent—you had better turn around, go the other direction, and understand that the only way you will ever know God, salvation, and forgiveness is by understanding that God has appointed a Judge who will judge all sinners. And that Judge is none other than Christ Jesus, who died on the cross as a sacrifice for sin, and whom God raised from the dead to affirm that His sacrifice was complete and sufficient." Romans 10:9 affirms "that if you confess with your mouth the Lord Jesus and believe in your heart that God has raised Him from the dead, you will be saved."

Natural man is ignorant. Even the most respected philosophers—the wisest of the wise, the brain trust of Athens, the most religious, rational, and most erudite—ended up as idolaters, groping around to find God. They had to repent or face eternal judgment from the one who offered them salvation through His death and resurrection.

## IGNORANCE IS NO EXCUSE

God will not leave those who have never held a Bible in limbo or some neutral position. There are no free passes. Look at 1 Corinthians 10:20 to shatter this heresy; Paul said that an idol itself wasn't really anything: "Rather, that the things which the Gentiles sacrifice they sacrifice to demons and not to God, and I do not want you to have fellowship with demons." Nothing the whole heathen world sacrifices to their supposed stone, silver, and gold idols is engaging the true God; it is engaging the forces of hell. They are linked with Satan and demons.

You might say, "Oh, those poor well-intentioned pagans! They're working their way toward God the best way they know how." No, they're working their way toward hell. They're connecting with demonic forces impersonating idols that don't exist. There are no other gods than the true God. People believe there are, because demons impersonate the gods they worship and do enough tricks to keep those people connected to their false deities.

It's not just a case of "Too bad they're ignorant." They're not in limbo, they're hell-bound. Ignorance is no excuse. Natural reason seeking God ends up ignorant, idolatrous, and demonic. Demons are behind all false religions. They are behind all philosophical and religious systems. They are behind every lofty thing lifted up against the knowledge of God. Any unbiblical, anti-God idea is demonic.

There's a dramatic illustration of this teaching in 2 John 9–11: "Whoever transgresses and does not abide in the doctrine of Christ does not have God. He who abides in the doctrine of Christ has both the Father and the Son. If anybody comes to you and does not bring this doctrine, do not receive him into your house nor greet him; for he who greets him shares in his evil deeds." If you deviate from what the Bible says about Christ—His birth, nature, life, substitutionary death, resurrection—you don't have God. If you don't know Jesus, or if you're even wrong about Jesus, you cannot know God. You're just engaging with demons.

People have asked me, "Is there a lot of satanic religion in our society?" Yes. Everything but true Christianity is satanic, to one degree or another, and in one manifestation or another. It's not that everybody worships Satan directly, though some do. But anybody who doesn't worship the true and living God through Jesus Christ, in effect, worships Satan.

I don't think you want to do that, because God gets very jealous. In Deuteronomy 32:21, God said, "They [Israel] have provoked Me to jealousy by what is not God; / They have moved Me to anger by their foolish idols." You don't want to provoke the Lord to anger, because you're not as strong as He is. You will lose.

Again, the best that man can do through his own reason comes up as foolishness, ignorance, and idolatry, and it engages the forces of hell. Romans 3:10 is the universal indictment of humanity: "There is none righteous, no, not one." Man's religions are "bad good." They may be good on the human level through emphasizing kindness or being charitable. But they are "bad good," because the motive is not to glorify God, and anything less than that is a wrong motive. People don't do good in the sense of righteous good that pleases God. In fact, they're wretched on the inside; their throats are like open graves. They open their mouths and out comes the stench of death.

Paul says of the law that "it stops every mouth" (see Rom. 3:19). Don't open your mouth and try to defend yourself. Don't say, "But . . . God . . . I tried. I'm a pretty good person, and You know I'm certainly better than the people over there." All that natural revelation does for you is make you accountable to God, and inexcusable. It shuts your mouth, and you have nothing to say, because in verse 20, your deeds, your works of the law—meaning your good deeds, your religious deeds—will never be justified in God's sight. You can't be good enough to get there on your own.

If you can be saved without the gospel, then salvation is by works. Nobody is going to be justified before God that way. There's only one way to be justified, and Paul went on to describe it in Romans 3:22: "The righteousness of God, through faith in Jesus Christ, to all and on all who believe." You have to come to

Christ; you have to believe in Christ. The only way of salvation comes in verses 23–24: "All have sinned and fall short of the glory of God, being justified freely by His grace through the redemption that is in Christ Jesus." The only way to be saved is by faith in Jesus Christ.

## REWARD AND RETRIBUTION

Second Thessalonians 1 gives a brief but very potent lesson in reward and retribution, beginning in verse 7: "The Lord Jesus [shall be] revealed from heaven with His mighty angels, in flaming fire." This is the Second Coming, the day Paul mentioned in Acts 17:31, on which God has appointed Jesus to be the Judge. On that day, God will reveal the Lord Jesus from heaven with His mighty angels in flaming fire and furious final judgment.

Notice an essential point in the next verse: "He will deal out retribution." Retribution means judgment, payment, punishment. For whom? For "those who do not know God, and [for] those who do not obey the gospel of our Lord Jesus Christ" (2 Thess. 1:8). In the original Greek, that passage is designed to be an explanation of those who do not know God. The word "and" would be better translated "even" because it's a further description of the same people. The passage could read this way: "This flaming final judgment falls on those who do not know God, by virtue of the fact that they do not obey the gospel of our Lord Jesus, and these will pay the penalty of eternal destruction away from the presence of the Lord, and from the glory of His power."

If you don't believe the gospel, you don't know God. If you don't know God, you're going to be judged without regard for your human morality.

Views of inclusivism, natural theology, or wider mercy are heresy. One writer called this perspective "later light," suggesting that this is new revelation that says when you die and go to heaven, what you don't know will get straightened out up there. Such a claim is frightening in its implications; it is a damning and deadly heresy, because God commanded us to reach people with the complete and true gospel. At any time, God may be using us as mouthpieces of His truth and a means by which others may hear and be saved.

God Himself is the only source of knowledge with regard to His own being and a relationship with Him. God, as the only source, must disclose it to us, and He has done so by the Holy Spirit. The Spirit knows the deep things of God, revealing them to the writers who recorded them in the Scriptures. Thus, in the inspired word of the Bible, and only there, we have the mind of God and the mind of Christ.

Natural theology reduces you to an ignorant idol worshipper, engaged with demons and headed for divine judgment. Natural revelation is sufficient to damn, but not to save. It makes man without excuse but not without condemnation. Our command and duty as responsible Christians is still in place: go into all the world. Mark 16:15–16 makes the mandate unmistakably clear: "Go into all the world and preach the gospel to every creature. He who believes and is baptized will be saved; but he who does not believe will be condemned."

## WHY BOTHER WITH THE TRUTH?

Even before you dedicate yourself to proclaiming the whole truth of Christianity, you face the question of whether or not witnessing and evangelism of any kind are worth the trouble. If the gospel is that hard to accept, and if God chooses His people anyway, why should you put yourself out?

To some people God grants His gracious Spirit, to work in them at an early age, so that they never doubt the necessity and urgency of salvation. Others come to an understanding of what the truth is gradually, over time. Still others can point to dramatic events in their lives when the power and importance of the gospel jumped out at them suddenly and gripped their hearts. And so it is that many of you, who have been Christians for some time, have been for the first time awakened dramatically by this book to the glory of the true gospel.

In an earlier chapter I wrote that meeting a beautiful cheerleader named Polly was one especially important event in my spiritual life. Another happened the summer after my freshman year at the university. I was thrown from a car going 75 miles an hour—this was before seat belts—and slid about 120 yards down an Alabama highway on my backside. I was fully conscious (I even stayed in my own lane!), and I tried to brake by putting my hands down. The scars on my hands are still there.

No one else was hurt, and a passerby took me to the nearest hospital. After the doctors there did what they could, they wrapped me up and put me on a plane home to California. I spent three months lying on my stomach and wondering if I'd ever play football again. I thought a lot about life and death, and what exactly we were on earth to do. I came to grips with the reality that life is fragile, and that I needed to make sure I was doing what the Lord wanted of me. It could all be over in a heartbeat, with no warning whatsoever.

Up to that time, I was more concerned with finding my own direction in life, and picking my own career, than listening to what God might want for me. But then life took on a serious tone. I realized I wasn't in control of my future. I had survived something that should have killed me; God suddenly had my undivided attention. I remember saying, "Lord, I'll do anything You want me to do, and I understand that life is much bigger than my little agenda."

Like a lot of healthy young college students, I'd felt a sort of invincibility and assurance that I was going to carve out my own little world. After the wreck, I began to come to grips with the reality of eternity, and what really mattered. I remember lying in bed, reading the New Testament, and thinking seriously about the things of God. I eventually healed, and the Lord allowed me to go on and enjoy an extensive athletic career, which was grace upon grace.

My introduction to Polly a short time later sealed the commitment. To know Him, to know His gospel, and to make it known became my life.

God calls all Christians to proclaim the message of Christ. Most do it by word and deed, as a part of daily living. Some make evangelism their lives' work, as God called me to do. I learned, early on, from that first experience at a South Carolina bus station down to the present, that I can't save anybody. All I can do is proclaim the gospel.

If you looked at the world and judged God's power by the responses of men, you would give up trying to share the Word of God. I have gone places and poured out my heart, and nothing happened. But that's all right, because all that the Father gives to Christ are going to come home. That's what Jesus said: "All that the Father gives Me will come to Me" (John 6:37).

I'm not responsible for who gets saved, and neither are you. I refuse that responsibility. Then who is responsible? "No man comes to Me," Jesus said, "except the Father draw him." God has that responsibility, not us. Therefore, I can look over the multitude and say, as Jesus said, "Most of you won't believe." But some *will* believe, brought to faith through reading the Bible, talking with a friend, or hearing a preacher on the street. Then, instead of being unbelievable and foolish, these words that are so hard to believe become the only balm that soothes a sinful heart; the only guide through the narrow gate that leads to eternal life; the only truth rich, complete, and holy enough to save a soul from eternal fire.

Those hard words become precious and welcome and treasured. "All that the Father gives to Christ, they will come."

They will come. Our calling is to reach them with the truth.

# NOTES

CHAPTER 1

1. Robert Schuller, *Self-Esteem: The New Reformation* (Waco, Tex.: Word, 1982), 64.
2. Ibid., 71.
3. Ibid., 76.
4. Ibid., 98.
5. Arthur Bennett, ed., *The Valley of Vision* (Edinburgh: Banner of Truth, 1975), introductory prayer.

CHAPTER 2

1. Michael Scott Bashoor, "Not Ashamed of the Gospel: Paul's Preaching of the Cross in a Shame-Sensitive Culture" (M.Div. thesis, The Master's Seminary, 1998), 43.
2. I'm indebted to Don Green for much of the material here and through page 29. His superb paper "The Folly of the Cross" is scheduled for publication in *The Master's Seminary Journal*, 2004 spring issue.
3. Martin Hengel, *Crucifixion* (Philadelphia: Fortress Press, 1997), 6–7; emphasis in original.

CHAPTER 5

1. John Stott, *Basic Christianity* (Downers Grove, Ill.: InterVarsity, 1958), 121.

CHAPTER 6

1. C. S. Lewis, *Mere Christianity* (New York: Macmillan, 1943, 1945, 1952), 110–11; emphasis in original.

CHAPTER 7

1. Arthur Pink, *An Exposition of the Sermon on the Mount* (Grand Rapids: Baker, 1951), 423; emphisis in original.

2. C. H. Spurgeon, "The Two Builders and Their Houses," February 27, 1870, in *The Metropolitan Tabernacle Pulpit* (Pasadena, Tex.: Pilgrim Publications, 1970, 1983) 16:128.

3. C. S. Lewis, *Mere Chrstianity* (New York: Macmillan, 1943, 1945, 1952), 171.

CHAPTER 8

1. Cited by T. R. Glover, *Poets and Puritans* (London: Methuen & Co., 1915), 110.

2. R. F. Delderfield, *The March of the Twenty-six* (London: Hodder and Stoughton, 1962), 197.

CHAPTER 9

1. William Barclay, *The Gospel of Matthew* (Philadelphia: Westminster, 1958), 2:10.

CHAPTER 11

1. *Los Angeles Times*, 9 December 2000.

2. Peter Kreeft, *Ecumenical Jihad* (Harrison, N.Y.: Ignatius Press, 1996).

3. This familiar quotation is often found in inclusivist literature. Some sources attribute it to an anonymous author. Others attribute it to various names. Most frequently liked as author is Max Warren, a British Missiologist. A thorough search failed to turn up the origional source.

# ACKNOWLEDGMENTS

Thanks to John Perry, who expertly translated the message of this book from sermonic form to the printed page; and to Robert Wolgemuth, whose advice and encouragement were essential in the final editorial process. I am indebted to Don Green for his helpful research on the significance of the cross. Much of the historical background on crucifixion in Chapter 2 was condensed and adapted from a paper he wrote. Garry Knussman spent hours proofreading manuscripts and documenting sources. His help was invaluable. And I'm thankful as always to Phil Johnson for his editorial assistance throughout the project.

# ABOUT THE AUTHOR

J OHN MACARTHUR is pastor-teacher of Grace Community Church in Sun Valley, California, president of The Master's College and Seminary, and featured teacher with the Grace to You media ministry. The author of numerous bestselling books, MacArthur's popular expository style of teaching can be heard daily on the internationally syndicated radio broadcast *Grace to You*. He is also the author and general editor of the *The MacArthur Study Bible*, which won a Gold Medallion award and has sold more than 500,000 copies. John and his wife, Patricia, have four grown children and twelve grandchildren.

For more details about John MacArthur and all his Bible-teaching resources, contact Grace to You at 800-55-GRACE or www.gty.org.

---

For more information on the high cost but infinite value of following Jesus, go to *www.HardToBelieveBook.com*.

---

# ALSO FROM
# JOHN MACARTHUR

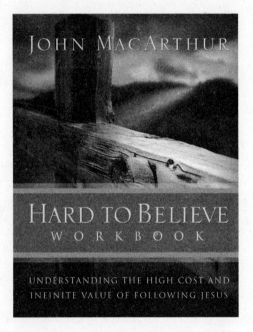

### *Hard to Believe Workbook*
In contrast to the superficiality of much modern Bible
teaching, Dr. John MacArthur uncovers in this workbook the unvarnished truth of what Christ really
taught. In simple, compelling terms, he spells out what
is required of those who would follow Him.
With provocative questions and exercises, he leads
readers to a full understanding of the call of Christ.

## Safe in the Arms of God

The death of a child is the most devastating experience parents can ever face. And a perplexing experience for their Christian friends and loved ones. But God has not left you alone with grief. With scriptural authority and the warmth of a pastor's heart, Dr. MacArthur examines the breadth of the entire Bible to highlight its many references to God's unfailing love for children and His assurance of their eternal safety.

ISBN 0-7852-6343-8

## Twelve Ordinary Men

Jesus chose ordinary men—fisherman, tax collectors, political zealots—and turned their weakness into strength, producing greatness from utter uselessness. MacArthur draws principles from Christ's careful, hands-on training of the original twelve disciples for today's modern disciple—you.

ISBN 0-8499-1773-5; workbook ISBN 0-8499-4407-4

## The Fulfilled Family

With traditional family values in decline and under assault, how can parents convey Godly principles and morals amid competing messages? John MacArthur takes a look at the strategy outlined in Ephesians 5 and 6. He says that the secret to a successful family comes down to questions that must start in the heart, such as: Am I committed to obedience to the Spirit of God?

ISBN 0-7852-6254-7

## Why One Way?

A concise guide to understanding how and why the ancient Christian faith makes sense for today and a blueprint for communicating truth to a "truthless" and cynical generation.

ISBN 0-8499-5558-0

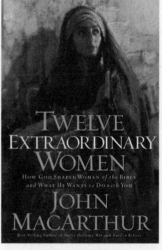

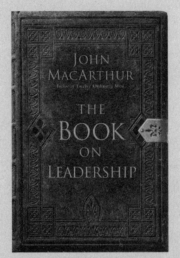